I0416911

Attachment:

The Social Foundation of a Successful Life

Dave Ziegler, Ph.D.
Executive Director
Jasper Mountain
Jasper, Oregon

Copyright © 2014 by Dave Ziegler. All rights reserved.

No part of this publication may be reproduced, stored in a retrieval system or transmitted in any form or by any method, photocopying, scanning, electronic or otherwise, except as permitted by notation in the volume or under Sections 107 or 108 of the 1976 United States Copyright Act, without the prior written permission of the author. Requests to the author for permission should be addressed to:

Jasper Mountain
37875 Jasper-Lowell Road
Jasper, OR 97438-9704

E-Mail: davez@jaspermountain.org
Website: www.jaspermountain.org

Cover Design: Michelle Perin
Cover Photo: ShutterStock and Michelle Perin

International Standard Book Number: 978-1503060708

JASPER MOUNTAIN
Hope for Children & Families

No greater help can be offered to another person

than to enhance their bonds of love and caring to others.

This book is dedicated to

those who help others grow deeper

in their interpersonal attachments.

Acknowledgments

It has been a joy to work over the last three decades with the devoted people who have made up the Jasper Mountain family. This unique organization has been so many things to so many people. It has been a place of healing for children, an opportunity to learn for students and family members, and a place of service to its employees. But regardless of how people have experienced Jasper Mountain, their lives were touched and would never again be the same. In the context of this treatment family/psychiatric residential treatment center/non-profit organization the information found in this book has been discovered first hand one child at a time. I want to thank everyone involved with Jasper Mountain, the Board of Directors, the staff, the volunteers, the individuals and businesses who support its work, and most of all the children who share their pain, their promise and their lives with us. The Jasper Mountain Board of Directors consists of Parke Blundon, Steve Cole, Gary Buss, Nji Nnamani, Debra Eisert, Linda Beach, Barb Lucas, Randy Nawalaniec, Chuck Davis, Mike Kelly, Frank Papagni, Rob Morris, Gene Heinle and the newest member Nathan Lichvarcik. Without this excellent Board of Directors there would be no organization and no success stories.

I also want to thank Judy Littlebury, Michelle Perin and John Ziegler who helped edit the drafts and offered very helpful suggestions. Finally, I want to thank two special women. First my mother, Rosemary Ziegler, who taught me about attachment so many years ago and instilled within me a deep understanding of what attachment is all about--even before I was able to put it into words, as I have tried to do in this book. Also my wife, Joyce, who in many ways reached out to me first. She has been relentless in enhancing my life in a special relationship that spans almost half a century, which includes 41 years of marriage. It has been from my mother and my wife that when I encounter someone who struggles with attachment that I know what they are missing in their life because I have been taught by these two women what attachment is on a physical, emotional, and spiritual level. There are no words to express my thanks for providing me with the social foundation that has made my life so successful.

Contents

Preface

This is the first of a series of books covering topics that parents, teachers and therapists struggle with every day in their attempts to help difficult children. The first volume, in what has been called The Success Series, covers attachment. First things first, why call this The Success Series? It is understood that any adult who has the challenge of working with a difficult child will want to succeed in this endeavor. But before going into the success for the adult, let us start at the beginning and first consider success for the child.

It may seem odd to hear this but, regardless of what you are running into with the child you are working with, the child is currently succeeding, but it is very possible that you are not. Of course, the measure of success for the child is different than it is for the adult. We adults want our children to be successful in social settings and school, developing and keeping true friends, giving and receiving support in the family, and overall reflecting positive emotions that are consistent with living a happy life. However, that is not the measure of success to the difficult child. It may be a bit different for every child, but I have noticed the themes are the same. The child believes he or she wins when the adult loses. Adults lose when they get angry, frustrated and make statements about giving up. Where we want them to fit in well, they want to set themselves apart; we want them to laugh and enjoy life, and they prefer to yell and disrupt any calm they find with a good tantrum. In other words, difficult children consider themselves a success when they succeed at what we would consider failing. This is the first of many excursions into the thinking of disturbed children that we will take together in this series.

The reason success for the disturbed child is measured by failure is complicated but, simply stated, it is because in the perception of the child what adults consider success is out of reach. There have been dozens, no thousands, of experiences where an adult has made it clear the child will not likely ever reach the top of the success mountain. The climb is difficult for any child, but what child will attempt to make the journey if he or she has been convinced that the result will simply be more failure? So what I am pointing out is that most adults miss the forest for the trees; they do not see how hard disturbed children work to succeed by their own definition.

Long ago I stopped telling these children to work harder because they were just not putting in enough effort. Take a closer look, they may be working harder than anyone to continue to disrupt, to tantrum, to make it clear to any and all adults that they are unlikely to fit into the mold we want them to fit into. Consider how much energy it takes to throw a respectable tantrum. Do you remember the last time you 'threw a wobbly' (Australian for tantrum)--not just getting upset but a fit that registered on the Richter Scale? This would usually mean real anger, some yelling perhaps, even slamming a door or throwing something. Now remember how tiring this was. Difficult children can do this several times a day (some several times an hour), and that takes a lot out of a person. But these children have years of training in preparation for the Olympic Tantrum Team, as soon as it becomes a competitive sport. I realize I am making light of something very serious to most adults, and I am doing so on purpose. Regardless of our challenges in life, if we cannot take an occasional step back to laugh at our situation and ourselves, then the issue has become greater than our ability to manage it. When this happens our internal confidence hits dangerously low levels, and we fall into a state some describe as "burnout."

But my point in starting with how successful disturbed children consider themselves is that most of these children have not given up; they try much harder than adults give them credit for. Many have all the makings of a champion, but the drive and energy just goes in the wrong direction. So I am suggesting we start from a place where we see the child as very committed, hard-working, persistent, and a tireless champion at failing in most areas that we consider success. But we must recognize this fact because we will want to redirect this herculean effort they have invested in their lives. To insure that most of us are on the same page, if you have a depressed, sullen child who does little or nothing, I would still include these children in the self-defined success camp. It is not a natural state for children to expend little external energy, sit in dark rooms and brood. Look at the effort it takes to fight the natural instinct to be interested in the world around them. But these children, whom I call the internalizers (contrary to the externalizers) must be worked with differently and can be more challenging than the aggressive and violent children. So consider that we do not have a child who is a failure; we have a child who is succeeding in all the wrong things. It may take some time before we help the child's brain realize that there is another way to succeed that brings even greater benefits.

Now we can return to the concept of success for adults. Having started with some insight that the children I have lived with for decades have taught me, just realizing that disturbed children do care and do put in considerable effort is the start to success for adults. This is because you will not succeed with a disturbed child unless you understand the child, which includes their inner world of contradictory thoughts and feelings.

We adults have a bad habit of measuring our success by how well our children perform on the measures we define as important. For example, the parent of a straight "A" student may have a bumper sticker on their car that appears to acknowledge the child, but before the child is mentioned it says "I am the proud parent of..." Who is really being recognized? Such parents often take pride in their skilled parenting even when their motivated and bright child asks for little academic assistance. However, the parent, who night after night works with the math-impaired children (an impairment to which I can personally relate) only to see a "C" on the report card, may struggle wondering if they are giving the child enough. I believe it is important to give credit where it is due, and I do not let busy professional parents off the hook just because their child does fine with little help. I also do not hold the parent of a struggling child responsible when the parent is working hard to help, despite the outcome.

We must start this Success Series with the understanding that to do our best is the best we can do. Therefore success as a parent is what we do and not what our child does. But let us add to our definition of success to improve our outcomes in preparing a child to have the potential at a future with social connections, with personal goals that are set and accomplished, and with a degree of personal contentment along the way.

We will cover a variety of topics in this Success Series, and each will add to the overall plan. These books will be short and to the point and are not intended to be exhaustive of the topic. If one of the topics is of great interest, then look into that topic more because there are many helpful resources. Before this series I rejected the notion of a book on a specific topic because the children I am writing about essentially never have just one problem area. My previous books have been about the whole child, although this theme will be continued in this series, there will be more attention given to a specific topic. I still believe that success will only come from treating the total child, and this means addressing multiple problem areas. After you have completed one or more parts of the Success Series and you find them helpful, then I suggest you consider reading some of my more comprehensive books that have a broader focus on the child. If you have not run into these books, they are:

Raising Children Who Refuse To Be Raised – This book takes a disarmingly frank approach to the most difficult behaviors and the most challenging children. It not only explains the causes of the most serious problems parents face, but it goes further to provide interventions that have been tried and found successful. Very serious problems such as aggressive, violent, explosive, hyperactive and belligerent behaviors are addressed in a practical and understandable way. Sections of the book are geared directly to parents and other sections to professionals with a suggestion that everyone read both so adults are working closely together to help these children.

Achieving Success With Impossible Children - Written for those who work with children who are the most troubled and challenging, and who are exceptions to all the rules. It offers practical applications and hands-on suggestions to help children become healthy successful individuals. Clearly written and infused with humor, it discusses working with difficult children in multiple settings such as during adoptions, in schools, with parents, and in residential care. It provides advanced intervention ideas including positive discipline and teaching responsibility. The message of the book is that success with very challenging children is not only possible but realistically achievable.

Traumatic Experience and the Brain, A handbook for understanding and treating those traumatized as children, Second Edition - This volume details the effects of childhood trauma on the developing brain and describes how early events in life rewire the person's perceptions of self, others and the world. It incorporates two decades of research on the human brain and answers the question, "So now what?" Now that we know a great deal more about how the brain works and how it is affected by trauma, what should we do differently to help traumatized individuals? Case examples help explain in understandable terms how we must work with the human brain and not work against it.

Beyond Healing: The path to personal contentment after trauma – This book takes a close, critical look at many of our beliefs about human limitations and offers a message of hope for those individuals who have paid such a high price for past abuse and trauma. Drawing on case studies, it provides a clear and realistic guide to reclaiming one's life after traumatizing experiences. The hope offered is based upon science and research and the writing style is accessible and down-to-earth. This book can be an invaluable guide to anyone who has personally experienced trauma or is attempting to help someone else who has.

Neurological Reparative Therapy, A Roadmap to Healing, Resiliency And Well-Being - This book provides a new model of treatment that integrates critically important components of brain functioning. This new integrated model is first brain focused (neurological) and stresses the healing (reparative) of adverse impacts that have prevented the brain from reaching its potential, and outlines a roadmap of an active process (therapy) in promoting healing, resiliency and overall well-being. The NRT model relies heavily on the research and professional literature of: brain development, trauma, attachment, and resiliency. The NRT roadmap identifies the best route to well-being through healthy brain development, attachment, and resiliency but relies on the helper to use his or her own skills, experience and techniques to take the journey.

I have only one goal for all of the above books, to help you succeed in working with difficult children and to learn from the journey. I have been blessed in my personal life and my professional career to have the very best of teachers, and I want to share what I have learned with you. So let us begin our journey with the starting point of remembering these basic things:

- Disturbed children are highly motivated to succeed in being a failure.
- We must measure our success not by what the child does, but what we do.
- Our own success will be linked with how well we understand the inner world of the child's thoughts and emotions.
- If we lose our sense of humor at any point in the journey, then parenting a difficult child will simply cease to be fun anymore, and this will put us on the road to burnout and failure.

Before we begin the journey I want you to know that you can do this. You can be successful with your difficult child. You may be saying, "How can he say this and mean it; he doesn't know me or my child!" Please consider that I do mean this, and I have worked with and lived with thousands of difficult children, many of whom would surpass your child for the future Olympic Tantrum Team. I have also worked with thousands of adults, from those with extensive experience to those with no experience at all, and helped them to be more successful. We know from psychology that two things help reduce the stress of a difficult challenge (and parenting a disturbed child is at the top of the difficult list). The first is having a plan of attack, and I will help you with this. The second is having confidence; if you lack confidence in yourself then for the time being accept my confidence in you. Now put aside your worry and your stress, and apply your energy to fully understanding the problems, and then come up with a plan that will improve your success at helping disturbed children.

Introduction

The study of psychology over the last hundred years can be compared to reading a book starting in the later chapters and progressively reading in reverse order to the beginning. Our understanding of the complex mind and psychological make-up of Homo sapiens has begun with adults, moved to young adults, teens, adolescents, toddlers and finally we are beginning to read with great interest the first chapters of life. As we have done this over the last thirty years, there have been continuous professional awakenings occurring as the antecedents of social, mental, and moral distress begin to tell their stories in very young children. The purpose of this book is to collect the blinding flashes of insight as well as the mundane aspects of research in order to begin to tell the story of how the patterns and organization of a human personality are established as an infant enters the stage, and what happens early in the first act. The theme of a person's story and, to a large extent, the fundamental success or failure of his or her entire life, is established in their early attachment and bonding with their environment.

We are just learning to understand very early childhood and the precursors to social and interpersonal success or failure. This is assisting us to see clearly how patterns of dysfunction in adulthood can be causally linked to the quality of very early attachment. In the last decade there has been considerable interest in the study of attachment between adults, and how quality attachment can make all the difference to a successful life. As important as adult attachment is, it all begins very early in life. Anyone who was deprived early on of a significant bond with a parent has been neglected in one of the most significant ways. Healing and the development of attachment can be repaired as will be shown in these pages, but not without tremendous effort and struggle.

As much as we currently know about this most fundamental of human interactions — attachment between two people — there is much we have yet to learn. For example, the developing study of genetics and epigenetics has just begun to add to our understanding of attachment. There will only be a brief reference in this book to how our genes impact our psychological and behavioral traits that support or prevent attachments. This is not because it is of little importance; it is because of how little we currently understand about a human being's predisposition to bond or not bond with a care provider. It is safe to say that the more we learn about attachment, there will always be much more to be learned.

I had a recent conversation with a child psychiatrist, and the topic of the discussion was the use of the diagnosis of Reactive Attachment Disorder. To my surprise the psychiatrist informed me that she did not use this diagnosis. When I asked her why she did not use a well-established diagnosis for children, she indicated that she did not find it to be helpful. She said many people misunderstood the diagnosis and its implications by believing it was a permanent condition, and there was little if anything that could be done. Therefore she felt the best approach was to avoid the issue entirely. In part I agreed with her. There is little doubt that many people misunderstand the difficulties of attachment and often believe there are no effective approaches to treating the problem. One way to approach helping children who struggle with attachment is to avoid the diagnosis entirely. However, this conversation with the child psychiatrist may be the best explanation of why this book was written. In my view a better way to address misunderstanding is to inform and provide more information. There is no question that problems with attachment are some of the most serious and pervasive early difficulties a child can experience, and moderate to severe social problems throughout life can be the result. Avoiding the issue because it is misunderstood does little to help a child with early attachment problems and who is on the verge of a sad and lonely life. Instead we must understand how these serious early difficulties occur, and more importantly, how to repair attachment as early in life as possible.

The fact is that attachment can be repaired. Although the dynamics of attachment can be explained in very complex neurological processes, both the problem and the solutions can also be explained in practical terms that nearly everyone can understand and implement. This is the goal of this book, taking the complex and making it both understandable and useable. It is to keep children from having a life that isolates them from the comfort, support and happiness that intimacy with other human beings can provide. It is difficult to imagine a full and happy life without healthy attachments with others. It is important to understand that having such healthy attachments is not beyond the reach of children with even the most serious cases of early disrupted connections with primary care providers.

I have been unwilling before now to write a book focused entirely on the issue of disrupted attachments. My thinking was that you cannot consider attachment difficulties in a vacuum. Children with disrupted attachment have multiple other issues. I decided to write this book now because I think we need both a more detailed explanation of what happens with the brain, and therefore what is needed to promote positive brain change regarding attachment, as well as the need for practical and effective ways to repair attachment.

Developmental psychology, child development and clinical application with trauma have all played important roles in a new understanding of attachment and bonding problems in early childhood. This book is broken into three parts. Part I discusses the important role that attachment plays in the future social success of children. It explains the tenets of traditional attachment theory and how trauma affects healthy attachment. This discussion continues with revisions to attachment theory that focuses on its historical weak points. A new theoretical view of attachment is proposed identifying the causes of attachment behavior. Part II breaks down attachment into a biological process and in particular neurological aspects of bonding. The foundations of social success are provided as well as how social dispositions are developed. With the understanding of what the problem is and how it develops Part III turns to clinical aspects of the treatment of attachment problems. Problems caused by trauma are identified, and the many therapeutic complexities are outlined. A model for treating attachment disturbances is proposed that discusses the clinical process in three distinct areas: disrupted attachment, anxious attachment, and no attachment. The book ends with a discussion of the prognosis for a successful outcome and projects time requirements for improving attachments in children.

Author's Note

If you are raising or working with a child who struggles with attachment issues, you have probably read a number of articles and books on this theme. So why take your time to read this book? I will offer two answers to this important question and both are related.

First, I have attempted to provide two facets to each issue throughout the book, a detailed description as well as a practical explanation. The practical is the more important because if this effort is successful then you will receive specific tools that work to help both the child and you. If I provide an in-depth analysis without providing you with ideas on how to address the problem, then the usefulness to you is diminished.

Second, the reason I can provide practical suggestions for the most challenging issues is the experience I have been blessed to have in my career. I will make a bold statement here because you may want to know the following. There may not be another individual who has been in the role of a psychologist and parent with as many children with attachment issues for as long a period of time as me. In the last 43 years I have parented and provided treatment to thousands of these young people, and they have been my teachers.

Your time is valuable, and I respect your need to make the best use of it. Therefore pick any section of this book and read a couple pages to see if you want to take the time to read the rest. If you do, I am confident that I can convey to you what I have learned from the children I have worked with—to assist you in facing your own set of challenges. If that is not the case, then email me at <u>davez@jaspermountain.org</u> and let me know.

Part I: Attachment Problems — Harmful Adaptation

How important is a secure attachment in setting the stage for personality traits and patterns of interpersonal and social success? The following quote by Mary Slater Ainsworth sums it up well:

> Securely attached [infants] are later more cooperative with and affectively more positive as well as less aggressive and/or avoidant toward their mothers and other less familiar adults. Later on, they emerge as more competent and more sympathetic in interaction with peers. In free-play situations they have longer bouts of exploration and display more intense exploratory interest, and in problem solving situations they are more enthusiastic, more persistent, and better able to elicit and accept their mothers' help. They are more curious, more self-directed, more ego-resilient – and they usually tend to achieve better scores on both developmental tests and measures of language development (Ainsworth 1979).

When the initial attachment between the child and the biological mother is disrupted and there is a measurable loss of the qualities mentioned above by Ainsworth (such as cooperative, positive, competent, sympathetic, enthusiastic and many more), the impact to the child can have life-long consequences. We can consider many of our society's most persistent and damaging social problems to be consequences of the disruption of early attachment. Among these are: crime, family disruption, substance abuse, depression and self-harm, child abuse and many types of toxic stress that eventually result in physical disease. The cost to our society of these personal and social problems is staggering. All these issues can be directly linked to early attachment and bonding deficits. I have previously written that perhaps the most important impact a professional therapist can have on a client is to help the individual improve the ability to attach to others. The more I understand the process and the influence of attachment, the more I believe this statement.

Some of the most severe problems with attachment are found with abused and neglected children. This is easy to understand since it is in the very early days and hours of life that the fundamental disposition of the child is established regarding reaching out to attach to a primary care provider, nearly always the mother figure. When this does not happen, for any number of reasons, the result is nearly always an impaired ability to bond with first care providers and later other people in general. Of these early problems the most negative result from early trauma, often consisting of the trauma of child abuse. When a child is harmed, and even more so when a child is neglected, the result produces formidable hurdles for the child to overcome immediately and throughout life. Individuals who do poorly in relationships can often trace social problems back to an early trauma history. Therefore trauma and attachment must often be considered together.

A starting point to this discussion is to consider what attachment is. Beverly James defines attachment as, "a reciprocal, enduring, emotional, and physical affiliation between a child and a caregiver" (James, 1994). In the evolutionary ladder of primates, research has shown the more advanced the species, the longer it takes to mature (Bowlby, 1982) and humans are at the top of this evolutionary ladder. The message encoded in our genetic markers is that Homo sapiens not only do better in a social network, but survival itself requires sophisticated levels of social interaction starting on day one of life, and from then on. The natural selection process has made humankind the most dependent of creatures on one another. The most successful humans are those who have close social networks throughout life. The social survival network that is first and foremost in importance is the attachment bond with one or more primary care providers.

Attachment is one area where we cannot ignore the fact that we are animals, and thus we have instinctual patterns leading to survival that involve social mechanisms. Bowlby describes the role of instinct in the process of attachment as, "a complex weave of survival and adaptability combined with fixed action patterns in a feedback loop with the environment" (Bowlby, 1982). The newborn human can do little or nothing to protect itself or promote survival other than one very important step--it can elicit an instinctual response from the mother to provide all basic needs for surviving and thriving. Without this essential interplay of child and mother, it is a wonder that human infant survival at birth is as frequent as it is. From a survival standpoint it would appear that a human has everything going against it. It has no form of self-protection, it has no ability to shield itself from the weather, it has no initial method of movement toward or away from either threats or comfort, and it has a large cranium that makes the birth process difficult at best and presents a challenge afterward because it weighs more than the baby's neck muscles can support. One aspect of the birthing process being difficult is a very large head then shoulders passing through the birth canal, but this disadvantage of a large head will eventually make all the difference. It will be this out of proportion brain that will eventually make the human being the most adaptable animal on the planet. However, without attachment the rest of human potential is very much in doubt for one of nature's most helpless of creatures at birth.

Since Bowlby's early work on attachment starting in the fifties, it has been believed that attachment and bonding may well be one of the essential keys to explaining the most fundamental human psychological and social problems. This is no longer a belief but an established fact. We now have significant research to confirm this global belief that a person's basic psychological disposition can be established very early in life. The way a child begins to understand his or her surroundings, what Bowlby called an "internal working model," has been found to influence a child's perceptions from early childhood into adulthood (Sroufe, 1986). Experiencing a supportive and responsive parent, the child develops the many attributes described by Ainsworth earlier. However, if the child runs into an unresponsive, uncaring or even abusive parent, the result is nearly always an internal working model of distrust and avoidance of all relationships, a topic that will be explained further in both Part II and Part III.

A brief overview of decades of research points out what we have intuitively believed for centuries--early attachment is critical to positive psychological development and social attunement. Starting with Ainsworth's research on child abuse, studies have shown the impact negative experiences have on the development of a child far into the future (Ainsworth, Blehar, Waters & Wall, 1978). Studies have shown that infants whose relationships with their mothers are more secure are more competent as toddlers, preschoolers and public school students (Belsky & Nezworski, 1988). The belief that attachment may have a generational dimension was given credence in a study that found that the history of nurturance the mother experienced in her own childhood predicted the quality of the attachment she developed with her own infant (Lewis, Feiring, McGuggog & Jaskir, 1984). Abusive mothers have been shown to be more emotionally sensitive to their infants than neglectful mothers, but less sensitive than non-abusive mothers (Crittenden, 1981). It has also been found that socially withdrawn children are more likely to come from insensitive mothers, and social withdrawal from peers predicts future social problems (Rubin & Lollis, 1988). Although the Rubin study focused on mothers who were insensitive due to a lack of awareness, there is a perhaps greater risk for children of mothers who are aware of what the child needs but do not respond. Research has shown a link between attachment insecurity and later behavioral problems (Erickson, Sroufe & Egeland, 1985). Foundations of social success were found in a study showing secure attachments predicted: more competence with peer relationships, a more positive disposition, higher levels of empathy, and having more friends as the child matured (Lewis, et. al., 1984). In yet another study, securely attached infants at eighteen months were more enthusiastic, persistent, cooperative and more effective (Matos, Arend, and Sroufe, 1978). The nature and quality of primary attachments have predicted socially meaningful characteristics in later life (Bates & Bayles, 1988). As you can see from the dates of these studies, we have known these factors for decades, and the above are just a few of the significant research findings over the last forty years in this area.

In psychology, as in medicine, we are much quicker to identify a problem than the causes or the solutions to the problem. It is clear that our society has many dysfunctional members. There are well over two million men and women in our jails and prisons, a higher proportion than any developed country in the world (Russia briefly surpassed the US in 2011 but once again we are back on top). The majority of men and women in our correctional institutions were originally children with disrupted attachments and many have lived a life of anti-social behavior beginning in childhood. Our drug and alcohol programs are full with waiting lists. Domestic violence, divorce and broken homes are at the highest level in our history. Poverty, unemployment and hopelessness exist in abundance in modern America. For the wealthiest nation on the planet, life in

America includes high rates of depression, dysfunction and shocking levels of hopelessness.

Although causative cultural phenomena can be identified in the masses, failure in our society is experienced one person at a time and one life at a time. How do some people beat the odds while others have the odds beat them? Some of the most exciting answers to this question are coming from the study of early dispositional patterns developed in childhood, or what can be called secure and insecure attachment. Bowlby addresses the importance of attachment in the following statement:

> A young child's experience of an encouraging, supportive and co-operative mother, and a little later father, gives him a sense of worth, a belief in the helpfulness of others, and a favourable model on which to build future relationships. Furthermore, by enabling him to explore his environment with confidence and to deal with it effectively, such experience also promotes his sense of competence. Thenceforward, provided family relationships continue favorably, not only do these early patterns of thought, feelings and behavior persist, but the personality becomes increasingly structured to operate in moderately controlled and resilient ways, and increasingly capable of continuing so despite adverse circumstances. Other types of early childhood and later experience have effects of other kinds, leading usually to personality structures of lowered resilience and defective control, vulnerable structures which also are apt to persist. Thereafter on how someone's personality has come to be structured turns his way of responding to subsequent adverse events, among which rejections, separations and losses are some of the most important (Bowlby, 1982).

How do we repair what has gone wrong with attachment, or are we destined to endure the life-long damage to individuals and to society as a result of disrupted attachment? It helps to know what we want to avoid and what we want to enhance, and then the challenge becomes how to do both.

Attachment Theory

The following is an extremely brief discussion of traditional attachment theory and can only touch on some of the major areas of a very complex topic. What is being called traditional attachment theory was first advanced by an English psychiatrist who was initially trained as a Freudian psychoanalyst. This psychiatrist, John Bowlby, who has already been quoted, had an initial goal in 1956 to explain the experience of loss and subsequent behaviors of very young children in Freudian terms. Like the early development of many breakthrough theories, Bowlby was not initially even looking at bonding specifically. But what he found in his consideration of childhood responses to loss was the connection between the child and the adult determined the experience of loss. From this beginning, research and clinical practice with children and with adults has steadily grown and in some ways in recent times is just now hitting its stride, fifty years after its beginnings.

Initially Bowlby, as well as other clinicians, had noticed in young children's response to loss that there was a somewhat predictable sequence of behaviors: first, the child protested with anger and rage, second, the child became depressed and showed despair, and finally, the child became detached from people and from the environment (Bowlby, 1982). One of the first methods to examine this behavior was research with primates. Researchers found that young primates gravitated to

21

auditory stimuli of low, familiar, limited range of magnitude sound and avoided stimuli of a high, irregular, and extensive range of magnitude. This indicated a young primate's preference for the predictable and calming over stressful chaos. When these animals were raised in extremely restricted environments, they would respond with two equally unproductive reactions--either approach all stimuli or avoid all stimuli. It was consistently found that when primates were raised in an environment where its evolutionary adaptations did not fit the environment, it would develop bizarre and, at times, non-survival behaviors (Bowlby, 1982).

Once again confirming that we are a part of the animal kingdom, primate research was subsequently replicated with humans with the same results. It was found that human attachment had a lot to do with the infant experiencing its needs being met and also how these needs were met. For example, being given a bottle to feed is qualitatively different than the touch, warmth and comfort of breast feeding with the mother (Bowlby, 1982).

As Bowlby's discovery work on attachment proceeded, he found no simple explanations for human attachment but a complex succession of increasingly sophisticated systems affecting attachment behavior. These included the following systems: instinct, physical, emotional and social systems.

Instinct

A major influence upon attachment is instinct. For Bowlby, attachment is as instinctual as any of our most fundamental drives such as survival and sexual gratification. The first instincts of primary importance are the instincts to survive, to be social, and to adapt to the environment. How these three instincts interact is as important as each are individually.

It makes sense that a newborn would have the instinct to connect to a source of protection and nourishment. But it is often overlooked that instincts arise in the mother as well. An infant appears to be predisposed or neurologically wired to attune to the voice, smell and face of the mother. In a similar manner the mother is instinctively predisposed to respond in a protective and nurturing manner to the child. Mothers are wired to develop an ideal level of proximity to the infant. However, not all mothers have strong enough instinctual drives, and the age, available support, previous history and environmental issues of the mother can be influential factors in this process. Studies with mothers have indicated that a young age of the mother and/or a low educational level signal risk factors in providing a nurturing environment (Sroufe, 1986). One specific example of the mother/child instinctive reciprocity is smiling, which in infants is reserved initially for a human face and voice. Smiling is one of the first vehicles of communication (Bowlby, 1982).

Despite the importance of instincts on attachment, these mechanisms are not tamper proof. Deviations in evolutionary adaptation, as Bowlby describes instinctive behaviors that don't achieve the desired results, can produce maladaptive behavior patterns. These patterns can include being at odds with the child's own best interests or even working against survival itself. Parents of children with attachment issues will find it familiar that these children can act against their own preferences or best interests. Bowlby believed that instinctive behaviors can be thwarted, which could make them revert back to more primitive behavioral levels or become cross-wired with their inherent purpose to promote reciprocal social bonding (Bowlby, 1982). In other words, a child may chronically push supportive adults away. When this occurs, a negative cycle develops with the child slipping further and further away from the instinctive goal of connection.

The Role of Fathers

A good friend read an early draft of this book and asked me a question many males have considered. He has four grown children and has been a very good father. His question was, "You give mothers a critical role in the attachment process, but what about us fathers?" Sorry dads, you are important in the child's life but in a different way than mothers and in more of a supporting role in the beginning. The exception to this statement is when the father is the primary care provider. Most often the child's primary connection is with the biological mother or the person in that role. Due to instinct, the child's brain must identify very quickly the one individual to align with in order to stay alive (protection, food, warmth, etc.). There are any number of individuals who can be in the role of that primary contact person: adopted mother, foster mother, grandmother, father, step-father, or an unrelated individual. Although in one sense the child's brain will connect with any primary source of security and nurturance, this does not mean that all individual connections are equal. There is a major advantage to the connection that the biological mother has that only she can have with the child. The child has just spent approximately nine months literally joined in a union with the biological mother, thus influenced by her moods, her level of activity, her eating habits, her stress level, and much more.

The early experience of oneness with the mother has the potential of a profound influence not only for attachment but also for a lifelong yearning for other experiences of oneness. We don't have conscious memories of being one with our biological mother but our brain remembers. It is interesting in this context that a fundamental principal of every major spiritual tradition is oneness with God, the creator or a higher power. This could be considered an instinctual drive on a spiritual level to bond and attach with the divine. Other experiences of oneness could include a desire to have a child, seeking emotional oneness by having very close friends, and the experience of physical oneness in sexual union. Early experiences of attachment can therefore be profound influences throughout life. Fathers are unable to have the early experience of physical oneness with the child in the same way as the biological mother.

Although not in the same way as mothers, fathers create an important bond with the child usually in a support role early on, and as the child matures the role of the father grows in significance. The mother's attachment is more driven by instinct but between 18 to 24 months the father's attachment (unless he is the primary care provider) becomes more important and is driven by interpersonal connection. Because of what drives the different attachments, it may be that a young person has a better relationship with the father, but even then the child may be more intrinsically influenced by the mother (deeper and stronger feelings both positive and negative). The gender of children is an issue as well but more on the relationship side than the intrinsic side. This means that close relationships develop with fathers and children of both genders but somewhat different with males and females. How the relationship develops has a lot to do with gender and cultural ways that dads connect with sons differently than daughters, particularly in adolescence.

So the best way to explain the different bond with mothers and fathers is to say they are both important but very different. It is possible that the father could bond better with the child than the mother. For example, the inconsistent biological mother may frustrate the child's brain and the child relies more on the father. It is possible that the older child may form a stronger relational bond with the father because of any number of interpersonal factors such as: personality, likeability, mutual interest, amount of attention, and other relational factors. Therefore fathers are not unimportant, particularly after the first two years. Fathers can be a very potent influence during the child's early years on learning skills to bond with others in relationships throughout life.

Physical, Emotional and Social Attachment

The three important components of attachment theory where bonding takes place are in the physical, emotional and social dimensions.

Physical factors influencing attachment involve aspects of human physiology including hormones and the central nervous system. The slow development of the pre-frontal lobes of the brain may have infants acting primarily on the pleasure principle enhancing attachment with the mother (Bowlby, 1982). The importance of physical touch and other senses have already been mentioned.   There are important physical components of neurobiology that will be discussed in some detail in Part II.

Emotional bonds are developed (or not developed) rapidly in infants and once established they are long lasting. Children either feel good or bad when they are emotionally close to adults.   The apparent role of emotions in the attachment process appears to assist in appraisal of both the infant's internal states and the external environment. Bowlby calls this affective appraisal intuition. Attachment is a two way street and emotional connections must develop on the part of the adult as well as the child. The lack of bonding on either end can result in tragic consequences for the child.

Social reciprocity is the purpose of attachment. To facilitate social behavior, early responses to stimuli become more discriminating with age — for example, an infant may initially respond to a picture of a face, then to a real face, then to a particular real face. Physical sensations combine with the infant's emotional/intuitive appraisal, producing behavior that is social or anti-social. Only if the child can accurately assess the affective state of another person can he or she productively participate in a social interchange (Bowlby, 1982). From early attachment experiences comes the ability to reach out and understand others or the reverse to avoid and misread the intentions of others.

Practical Application of Attachment Theory

Attachment theory that has come from Bowlby's work has been primarily defined in behavioral terms and can be summarized in eight important steps: 1) Social responses are first elicited by a wide array of stimuli, then this gradually narrows and after several months becomes confined to one or more individuals, 2) A bias develops to respond more to certain kinds of stimuli than to others, 3) The more experiences of positive social interaction with a person, the stronger the attachment becomes, 4) Exposure to human faces produces discrimination in the attachment figure, 5) The timing of attachment is critical and needs to develop during the sensitive period within the first year, 6) The sensitive phase begins sometime after six weeks (this position has subsequently been challenged), 7) At the end of the sensitive period, the infant responds to non-attachment figures with a fear response, making it difficult to attach after one year, and finally 8) Once a child becomes strongly attached, he or she prefers this person over all others despite separation (Bowlby, 1982). These eight steps have been modified over time with a general acceptance that the instinctual bond forms very quickly on a neuro-biological and social level.

Bowlby breaks attachment behaviors down into minute details. He addresses the important roles of crying, smiling, clinging, feeding, signaling, approaching, greeting and maintaining proximity. All these can be used to observe a developing bond. There are also disruptive behavior patterns that can develop which are contrary to the attachment process. The very early affective or intuitive appraisal of the environment develops default states or "set points" by which situations are measured. When set points are maladapted due to early disruptions, parental bonding behaviors may be met with anxiety, alarm, and anger (Bowlby, 1982). In these cases what should be emotionally and physically comforting to the child is reversed and closeness is anxiety producing and painful.

A variety of other behavior patterns can develop problems. Early negative experiences with hunger, illness, separation, unhappiness and pain can produce disrupted bonding. If an infant's signaling is not responded to in either sufficient quantity or quality, withdrawal can occur. Children have egocentrism, which means that after twelve months of age, they often construct their own internal world, and can ignore exterior information that contradicts their perceptions within this internal world (Bowlby, 1982). The child's right hemisphere develops very early to become aware of the interpersonal responsiveness of the parent. If needs are not met, then the habitual disposition develops negative predictions about being close to adults.

Infants have predictable responses to separation of the attachment figure. When separations are short, the reconnection is usually rapid. However, longer separations can produce anything from distress, to the child rejecting the attachment figure (Bowlby, 1982). Such behavior as a child ages can give some clues to what may have taken place very early in life and long before the child would have explicit memories (memories we are able to recall).

Attachment problems are frequently found in abused children for good reason. The interplay of trauma and attachment can be seen with these children. Research studies have found several important outcomes after trauma: abused children show significantly more frequent assaultive, harassing and threatening behaviors, they can respond to friendly overtures either by avoiding interaction or by mixed avoidance and approach, and they alienate and avoid adults who might help them, which can develop a self-perpetuating cycle (George and Main, 1979). As is often the case with social research, any parent with a child with attachment issues could have told the researchers this information and saved them some time.

For the heroic foster and adoptive parents who put themselves in harm's way by bringing an abused child into their home, the connection between early trauma and poor attachment is a daily challenge. It is helpful to go into more depth to provide a clearer understanding of this connection and to assist in repairing the damage to the child. Attachment Theory can assist with this task.

Adding an Understanding of Traumatic Experience to Attachment Theory

Some parents or caregivers may want to skip the initial descriptive section—they just want to know how to fix the problem. However taking the time to more fully understand the dynamics of trauma and attachment will pay off when we move the discussion to repairing disrupted attachment.

Traumatic experiences are those that override the ability of the individual to cope with the situation. The human brain is instinctively preset to consider traumatic experiences above all others. This is critical to accomplish the brain's primary goal of ensuring survival. Early experiences of deprivation of any basic needs will quickly signal the brain that there is an imminent survival threat. Clearly the importance of early support and protection for the human infant, combined with the mutual instinctive drives of child and mother, set the stage for the human race to be fundamentally social and interdependent. The ability and quality of developing attachments very early in life predict social success and personal happiness throughout life. In Part II these detailed neurological processes will be explained.

There are many factors that can disrupt attachment and start the individual on a long and lonely road throughout childhood and beyond. Some of these disruptive factors can include socioeconomics, the young age of the mother, substance use or abuse during pregnancy, domestic violence, mental and emotional health of the pregnant mother, to name a few. It appears clear that while attachment is critically important and humans are preset to bond, attaching to a primary care provider is also fragile. Perhaps the most damaging factor negatively influencing attachment is early traumatic experiences. Decades of research has shown that abused and neglected children are more likely to show avoidance of their mothers and resistance to the mother after even a brief separation (Belsky and Nezworski, 1988). Abused children have also been found to be more difficult to raise, while neglected children are more passive, and children in supportive environments are more cooperative (Crittenden, 1981). One study dating back to the 1980s resulted in the ominous conclusion that anti-social children become adults with disproportionately high rates of alcoholism, accidents, chronic unemployment, divorce, physical and psychiatric illnesses and welfare involvement—some of the definitional characteristics of our societal casualties (Caspi, Elder & Bem, 1987).

In the decades since the 1980s the research findings have continued to support the theme that attachment is critical to social success in relationships. Considerable research has been done over the last twenty years on the impact of children growing up in Eastern European orphanages. The results indicate what would be expected that the understanding and ability to attach among these children is generally impaired often to a serious degree (Zeanah, Smyke, Kigo & Carlson, 2005). In related research the children in such orphanages were found to be indiscriminate in their contact with adults even if they had parents (Zeanah, Smyke & Dumitrescu, 2002). Similar disturbances of attachment were also found in poor early care in family settings (Zeanah, 2000).

Research findings on the impact of poor attachment on the development of social relatedness has been consistent for over three decades. There are many essential skills that are needed to form effective bonds with others including parents, friends and intimate partners. Children with poor attachment have been found to lack the ability to understand the feelings and experience of others (Steele & Steele, 2008). Impaired social abilities can at times lead to serious social deficiencies and even mental health disorders such as personality disorders (Fonagy, 2000).

On the other hand children with secure attachments have been found to be more socially active, positive and popular at school age, and tended to report less social anxiety than children with insecure attachments (Bohlin, Hagekull & Rydell, 2000). Securely attached infants have been found to be more able to be resilient by experiencing less anxiety when facing family stress early in elementary school (Dallaire & M. Weinraub, 2007). A study from Israel found that children with secure attachment were better adjusted in school with higher functioning in academic, emotional behavioral and social areas, and had higher social status among peers (Granot & Mayseless, 2001). Research has also found that children with secure early attachments view themselves more positively than those without such early bonds. Specifically attached children feel worthy of care and affection and are more likely to trust others and are invested in relationships with others (Laible, 2007).

The question of long-term impacts of early attachment problems is a clear area of concern addressed in research. As would be expected the impact of poor early attachment has been found to negatively impact friendships and intimacy with more impact coming the older the child becomes (Belsky & Cassidy, 1995). This makes logical sense because the social demands on children grow exponentially and are more complex as the child progresses from elementary school to secondary school and into teen years (Schneider, Atkinson & Tardif, 2001).

The quality of attachment and its impact on behavioral problems has also been the subject of research, and once again the findings are predictable. Depressive symptoms in mothers were found to be associated with behavior problems in young boys and girls with the problems showing up first in the females (Shaw & Vondra, 1995). Early attachment disruptions have consistently been found to be a risk factor in developing serious antisocial behavior (Van Ijzendoorn, 1997).

This small sample of data coming from research on attachment is very consistent with the vast amount of other research findings. It makes intuitive sense that early bonding difficulties and trauma would seriously impact attachment afterward. The major task of the brain is to promote survival, and thus the brain would instinctively move toward attachment. But when attachment provides not support and nurturing but pain and threat, then it makes sense that the brain would instinctively move away from attachment, and that is exactly what it does. Trauma can have a significant impact on the perceptions and disposition of the person toward connecting with others. Once again the brain's job is to keep track of past experience, specifically experiences that have represented a threat. The brain does this within the hippocampus where implicit memory is stored, also called trauma memory. Short-term memory comes and goes as needed. For example, you check into your hotel and it is room 1142 on the 11th floor. You don't want to come back after dinner and try to get in the wrong room so remembering the number is important. But a week or even a couple days later you will likely not remember this room number because it had only temporary importance. This is not the case for traumatic memory. Any threat the person has experienced must be effectively stored for later self-protection, and there is no shelf life to traumatic memory.

The brain gives special attention to memories of threats and traumatic experiences and encodes this information in the limbic region of the brain as implicit memory, meaning it is independent from conscious recall. If an experience in life reminds the hippocampus of a past threat, its job is to immediately contact the amygdala and sound the alarm, and no conscious thought is needed. This is the neurological explanation of Posttraumatic Stress Disorder (PTSD). One symptom of this emotional disturbance is intrusive recall and avoidance of certain stimuli. When the individual has difficulty functioning in life because of uncontrolled reactivity to sights, sounds and other stimuli, then PTSD can be the cause. Avoiding attachment, due to past trauma, is essentially PTSD with relationship and connection with others being the triggering stimuli. More impacts of trauma will be covered in Part II.

Bowlby's theoretical treatment of attachment remains the most complete and influential viewpoint many decades after it was first published in 1969. Few theories hold up over time without moderate to substantial modification and alteration. Bowlby's theory is somewhat of an exception, but it did have initial flaws. Perhaps the biggest flaw in traditional attachment theory is its exclusive emphasis on behavior. Attachment behavior was later to be recognized as the outgrowth of attachment and not the attachment itself. Bowlby himself acknowledged this by pointing out his initial, "failure in the first edition to make clear the distinction to be drawn between an attachment and attachment behavior" (Bowlby, 1982). Ainsworth goes a step further to point out that no behavior in and of itself can be called attachment behavior. Ainsworth has also offered three classifications of attachment behavior to more clearly define behavioral traits. These three classifications have received significant research attention: A) insecure avoidant, B) secure, and C) insecure resistant (Ainsworth, et. al., 1978). Crittenden later added two new classifications which are avoidant ambivalent and compulsive compliant (Crittenden, 1981). Research with these many classifications have centered around the use of a procedure developed by Ainsworth called the "strange situation" (Ainsworth, et. al., 1978). This involves putting the child in a controlled situation without the mother, then introducing a stranger and assessing the behavior.

Although this procedure has been a research standard for many years, its value in clinical application is not without controversy (Greenspan and Lieberman, 1988). Over the years even more complex classifications of attachment problems have been proposed. Later in the book I will suggest that these many categories be simplified to be more practically useful.

Traditional attachment theory initially confused the dependence of human infants and how long they take to mature, with their ability to attach. It was believed that humans took longer to form attachments than less advanced primates. Bowlby originally stated that the period of time may be many months to one or two years before the infant can be said to have attached (Bowlby, 1982). Research in developmental psychology has now shown that attachment usually begins at birth (Lieberman & Pawl, 1988) and some, including the author, would argue even before birth. Knowing that attachment begins very early is important when looking at the early experiences of children with disrupted attachment.

It is not surprising that attachment theory has needed revision. What is surprising is the degree to which it has been supported by research in much the same version as originally presented. With the intensive focus on child trauma over the last few decades and its influence on attachment, it is possible to take attachment theory a step farther.

Throughout Bowlby's descriptions of behavioral systems of attachment and bonding, there are hints of additional important aspects of human attachment other than behavior. Restricting the discussion of attachment to behavior does not assist in identifying the causes of the behavior and is of limited value in treating and repairing attachment problems. Recent work on the origins of attachment has pointed to the need to find an explanation that is not limited to behavioral factors and incorporates and weaves together such themes as instinct, intuition, emotions, learning theory and the experiences the child has with the environment.

A more holistic understanding of the many ways attachment is experienced can be said to include four principal areas:

Physical, Affective, Inter-personal, and Spiritual. These are the four ways a child can experience attachment. All of these areas have behavioral manifestations, but go much deeper than behavior and, in fact, can be said to cause the observable attachment behavior so clearly identified by Bowlby.

Physical – the infant is preset by instinct to operate on the pleasure/pain principle. What provides pleasure is pursued and what produces pain is avoided. What is pleasurable to an infant is warmth, touch, sweet food intake, and stimulation in the right amount. What is painful is isolation, unpleasant sensation, sour or spicy food intake and touch that irritates or hurts. With just this amount of information can be seen how the individual develops a disposition to approach or avoid that which provides pleasure or provides pain. Starting at birth, either the child's many basic needs are met or they are not. The child learns very quickly that to be interconnected to the mother/father is pleasurable or painful. A series of negative physical experiences, regardless of the cause, may produce disrupted set points (emotional dispositions) that endure long after the pain is gone. Examples can include medical treatments, deprivation caused by extreme poverty, or the most common cause being the many forms of child trauma. Children who experience physical pleasure from connection usually grow up to pursue warmth, physical touch and comforting stimulation of many types. However, children who experience initial pain from connection with others often develop into children who prefer to be alone, avoid touch because it can be irritating stimulation, and can even have a high pain tolerance and almost seem to prefer what most children would consider painful stimuli.

Inter-personal – related to a spiritual bond, inter-personal connection begins before birth and infants are wired to receive pleasure from the attachment figure. This creates a neurobiological disposition to experience pleasure from human closeness that will be explored in Part II. Initially the child with a healthy bond experiences no barriers between the self and the other person. As the experience gradually develops of separateness, or where the infant stops and the attachment figure and rest of the world starts, the infant experiences all interaction as inter-personal. At this level, instincts are in sync with the positive experiences of being interrelated with the other person producing pleasure, which includes positive neuro-transmitters such as dopamine as well as positive emotional states. This produces a social disposition that can continue for life. When early experiences produce distress and negative emotional states, particularly anything the child's brain considers a threat, then the traumatic associations to being connected inter-personally to others results in anxiety and stress. If a negative association is made in the brain to connection with another person, then this early experience can produce a life-long anti-social orientation where social connection is not pleasurable or stress reducing, but instead painful and stress producing.

Affective – affective states or emotions are complex neurobiological combinations of brain pathways that combine memory and perceptions or internal working models. The child has an experience that must be screened by the brain to determine if it is a potential source of threat or a source of safety. After this initial and very basic decision, then the child responds to the stimuli based upon past experience, and the result is a positive, negative or neutral emotional response. Decisions that form perceptual models are formed very quickly and they can be very enduring. An early perception of an adult as a threat can have life-long ramifications, and can form the approach or avoidance response. The child's intuitive appraisal of the environment combines perceptions that include the spiritual, the inter-personal and the physical into an emotional response to the person, the situation or to the environment overall. Fundamentally, it feels good and pleasurable to be attached, or it feels anxious, frustrating, and bad. The affective response stems from the first three areas above and is expressed in behavior of varying strength and intensity. Emotions play a key role in attachment and ultimately are the main determinates of a fulfilled life based upon the presence or absence of happiness, which is experienced on the affective level.

Spiritual – this can be described as the experience of oneness. Perhaps the most profound experience humans have is being one with another person. This experience comes before we have explicit memory, but our brains remember it well. At first this experience of oneness is experienced on a physical level when the child does not have the awareness of separateness from the mother. This experience is part instinct and part intuition and emotion. It is deeply felt by the child in a way that sets the stage of hopes and desires the rest of the individual's life. The infant does not have a context to fit this experience into, oneness is the context. Without this early experience setting the stage of connection, no amount of material possessions, power and influence or the adulation of others can fill the void deep within the individual. The memory of the deeply spiritual experience of oneness can be viewed as one component of the existential and spiritual searching later in life to find answers to the most profound questions of existence. The search to return to the experience of oneness is a major part of human longing that plays out in the search for meaning, religious pursuits and other relationships throughout life.

For infants the first experiences are of a state of being one with the mother, then having experiences with the mother and others, progressing to an internal world that includes developing beliefs and eventually developing values. This core experience of feeling connected or belonging to an ever expanding network of "I Thou" relationships can be called the individual's primary orientation to a social world. A successful early experience of oneness will become the brain's context for desires, hopes and searching throughout life. If the spiritual attachment process is halted at any stage, the result in the individual is permanently arrested development of their social orientation unless there are specific and effective interventions, which will be the focus in Part III.

Understanding these four ways that children experience attachment, as well as the behavioral manifestations of each, begins to give a blueprint of how healthy attachment or attachment difficulties develop. How these four components of attachment can be used to understand and to rehabilitate attachment and bonding, particularly in traumatized children, is the topic of Part III. Before moving to repairing attachment, Part II will address how attachment is experienced and how it impacts the brain.

Dave Ziegler

Part II: Attachment and Neuro-biology

There are many ways to consider attachment and one perspective that provides a biological understanding of the inner workings of the process is neuro-biology, or what is going on within the brain of the individual. The brain is key to both understanding the success or failure with attachment, and it is key to supporting continued success or mitigating failure. An understanding of the brain assists with a practical explanation of the many deficits that often accompany attachment disruptions. In Part II the goal will be to provide an understanding of attachment on a biological and neurological level. Although neuro-biological processes are the most complex topic in the understanding of attachment, these processes can be explained in straightforward terms and can add to an appreciation of attachment problems and inform some solutions to repairing attachment. Understanding social interactions and motivations of human beings must begin with an understanding of the brain.

The Brain's Priority on Survival

Survival is instinctively preset in the brains of all animals. All animals have some means to assist with survival. Some blend in with the surroundings, some rapidly develop locomotion to escape danger, and some can signal threat to a predator in a way intended to discourage an attack. However the human infant can neither blend, escape nor produce any effective level of deterrence. What the human infant is able to do, and in a quite sophisticated way, is use processes within its brain to appraise the situation and initiate instinctive responses allowing the child to adapt to threats. But unlike much of the animal kingdom, human infants must rely on adults for survival. The best the child can do is to sound the alarm and hope there is a rescue coming from an adult. Because the brain is hypersensitive to threats, the vulnerability in early years is very much recognized as the brain appraises the environment. For children who do not find an adult to provide safety and other basic needs, the sense of vulnerability may become a major trigger as the child matures.

Attachment and instinct are so intertwined that of three primary instincts at birth all involve attachment—survival, connecting to a care provider, and adapting to the environment. Instincts and early attachment are very hard to separate because both have the very same goals—to survive and to thrive, and the only strategy to meet these goals is to connect to a source of what the infant needs for survival.

From the very beginning, it is the brain that determines whether the individual will first survive and then thrive to any significant degree. So the newborn child must use brain power immediately rather than other forms of protective survival mechanisms. Some of these immediate brain skills include visually scanning the facial features of the mother to very quickly tell her apart from dozens and even hundreds of other similar faces. The brain must be able to identify the source of its protection and care. The child must form neural networks to remember the mother's smell. The child must also form a 'call and response' instinctive pattern with the mother that includes auditory sounds that elicit auditory and behavioral responses. Without each of these brain mechanisms, the child is not assured of knowing who is the source of all aspects of continued survival—food, protection, warmth, and all other basic needs; none of which the child can provide for him or herself for years into the future. There is nothing more important than survival to the infant's brain and, therefore, there is nothing more important than developing a strong connection to the source of protection and assurance of survival through the sending and receiving of basic needs. A child cannot choose to reject a primary care provider; the brain will not allow this. Only when the child's brain perceives the adult as a threat rather than a source of nurturance will rejection come into play. In the same way, a child cannot choose to bond with an adult who represents a threat to the child's brain. Once again, survival is too important and the brain will not allow the attachment.

Attachment begins as the most egocentric of motivations, meeting personal basic needs at all cost. But attachment has the potential to eventually become the source of the most selfless of motivations, even overriding self-preservation in giving one's life for another person. It is the process of how attachment impacts the brain that provides the foundation of the complex social network that humans create. In the beginning motivations are instinctual and primitive, but as the brain matures through attachment experiences, the most complex regions of brain growth are promoted.

The human brain is shaped by a number of factors and each will play an important long-term role in the quality of life for the individual. The primary shaping factors of the brain include: genetics, nourishment, physical care, stimulation and environmental experiences. Of these factors, four are directly influenced by attachment and the other is indirectly influenced.

Genetics – As the study of genetics becomes more sophisticated the resulting information is showing that what is considered our nature, or what is passed on to us by Deoxyribonucleic Acid or DNA, is more influential than previously believed. It is not only our physical body, such as the color of our eyes, that is determined by genes but our mental potential, our emotional disposition, and a host of other factors that were believed to be solely determined by environmental influences. One of the best sources of genetics information comes from twin studies and the findings have been amazing. Individuals with the same genetic makeup but raised separately have shown many more similarities than differences in personality, preferences, and social status. Coming soon in our future will be the ability to determine which genetic codes will be emphasized and which will be suppressed, a field known as epigenetics.

Nourishment – As a basic need, there is no substitute to the nutritional building blocks of healthy development. Children who do not receive the nourishment they need to grow strong and fully develop can have short-term and long-term serious negative impacts. Some of the environments with the most severe deprivations have shown growth deficiencies that can vary from minor to severe, even causing death. But children with severe deprivation of nourishment may not fully recover even when they are restored back to physical health. There have been studies finding long-term emotional scars as well as genetic dispositions that can be passed on for up to three generations (Jablonka & Raz, 2009). Insufficient nourishment can result in smaller physical size, smaller skeletal frame, smaller brains, and poor brain development as well as poor internal brain communication.

Physical Care – The nurture side of the nature/nurture framework of brain development has always been viewed as fundamentally important. Much of the discussion of attachment hinges upon the quality of care the infant receives. The physical experience of a child will signal to the brain how it can and must adapt to the environment it experiences. Physical touch, warmth, soothing, and addressing any physical discomfort are all signals to the brain as to how to adapt to care providers and the larger environment. The first language of a child is physical touch. If contact with others produces pleasurable touch or painful touch, the brain is prepared to adapt and respond accordingly. It was a major mistake in the past to believe that very young children do not remember the pain of their early experiences. In fact, early painful experiences do more to impact the developing brain than later painful events. Due to the pleasure/pain decision tree within the developing brain, early pain signals a survival threat that is imprinting upon the limbic brain region and will be remembered by the brain's implicit memory for life. Knowing the importance of pleasurable touch has helped with the care of newborn infants in hospital settings and overall medical care. After the child is born, the first priority should be immediate physical contact with the mother.

Stimulation – In addition to physical care, interpersonal or emotional care in the form of parent/child interaction is also critically important. A human being is not simply a repository of nourishment and physical needs. For healthy brain development to proceed from more primitive brain regions to more complex regions, neurons must connect and grow stronger in the only way they can—activation caused by stimulation. The child who is not stimulated will have significant neurological deficiencies, regardless of whether all other needs are met. A major way the child's developing brain is stimulated is within the interplay of communication between the parent and the child; therefore, once again attachment is critical to brain development.

Environmental Experiences – Once thought by some to be the only influence on the brain, we now know nurture is one of many influences, but a critically important one. The brain picks up messages from the environment and then adapts to these messages. Early positive or negative experiences can become the foundation for the child's emotional set-points, disposition, perceptions and early personality development. The child's brain is remarkably prepared at birth to respond to the signals it receives, and this ability is the child's best self-protective skill.

Many environmental experiences profoundly impact the individual before explicit memory, primarily found in the undeveloped neocortex, is well developed. It is common to be aware of strong reactions, likes and dislikes, without understanding the cause. Often the answer can be found in childhood experiences that only our implicit memory (that cannot be consciously accessed) is aware of. Our life experiences are critical to the development of the individual.

How the Brain Does Its Job

There are very powerful neurological processes within the child's brain that must be ready to work at a very sophisticated level immediately at birth. Actually, the brain does not wait until birth to operate on a very complex level. Once the brain is activated in the womb, it will work non-stop for the life of the individual and will never be able to be switched off. The brain is taking in sensory information and forming perceptions before being physically separated from the mother at birth. The importance of experiences of bonding before birth is sometimes overlooked, but can be very important. There are many factors that can harm the fetus and form a perceptual pattern of threat before the child is born. For example, ingestion of drugs can cause the child discomfort and agitation; excessive activity can disrupt the child's ability to rest and experience comfort rather than chaotic stimulation. Loud noises, intense anxiety on the part of the mother and many other factors can produce a brain that is struggling to adapt to pain rather than pleasure. And all of the above could take place within the womb. The child's brain is making appraisals of the immediate environment even before birth. It is important to acknowledge this both to prevent early negative experiences for the child and to understand how very early issues, at times, can create lasting perceptions in the child's intrinsic memory.

The brain does its work through a complex process of neuronal activity from a single cell to networks of billions of cells. The human brain is the most complex organic structure in the known universe with 100 billion neurons with the capacity of trillions of synaptic interconnections, and this does not consider the brain's glial or support cells. The resulting active components of the brain produce astounding numbers of working parts that are difficult to comprehend, even for the human mind itself. Each neuron performs complex processes that receive chemical signals, switch these to electrical charges that run the length of the cell and then return again to a chemical signal transfer to the next cell. This intricate process can take place through millions of cells at a speed faster than a Formula One race car at full speed. Essentially everything a person knows, senses, remembers and does is a result of the interconnection of neurons in the brain.

The brain is performing thousands of actions at any one time and it must prioritize its vast resources, and nothing is a higher priority than survival. This is one explanation for the fact that a child's brain is three times more active than the brain of an adult. There is no time to lose for the brain to take in information from the environment and insure that what it needs will be available in a consistent, predictable way through a primary connection with another person--what we call attachment.

The Neuro-biology of Attachment

Like everything else related to human behavior, attachment is essentially a function of neuronal activity. What takes place in the brain concerning attachment will play a major role in the structure and function of the social brain. Both the positive contributions of attachment as well as the problems from a disrupted attachment are brain-based. For example, there is a neurological explanation for many deficiencies related to self-regulation, resiliency, stress management and empathy. There will also be neurological explanations for stress reduction, relaxation, and even empathy. Very early in life the level of attachment will determine how the young brain performs neuronal functions such as appraisal, interpretation and regulation of social and emotional information (Schore, 2003). Our perceptions are also developed very early and these early views of the environment can have a lasting influence upon the individual throughout the life span. This is a partial explanation for why children with disrupted attachment seem to think in illogical ways that seem to defy reason or purpose.

Use-dependent development of brain cells can be seen very clearly with attachment. When neurons attach to other neurons and are stimulated, not only the individual brain cell grows in size and strength but the network the cell is a member of does as well. The brain cells that are stimulated and exercised are the ones that stay active and healthy, whereas neurons that are not used are "pruned" through atrophy and eventual cell death called "apoptosis." The brain regions that would normally be prepared to respond to the care provider with attunement and an interplay of positive, reciprocal interactions will die if they are not stimulated. However, the stress- related arousal caused by a lack of attunement with the mother will now develop instead, and become more potent in handling perceptions and future social connections in a less than positive manner. Therefore, attached children become better over time with attachment and unattached children will not improve without impactful experiences that change the brain's perceptions. Due to the habitual nature of the way the brain processes information using the most developed neural networks, it is important to provide experiences that repair attachment as young as possible. The brain is a marvel of efficiency and it will process information using its most developed neural maps.

In the same way that we follow the same route to frequently visited locations without giving it much thought, the brain uses well-developed pathways in the brain because this is the most efficient way to operate. The result is habitual thinking, habitual emotions and habitual behaviors. The role of well-developed neuro-pathways will be a major aspect of the persistent and long-term implications of positive or negative early attachments. This is an answer to the dilemma of parents when they wonder why a child repeatedly does something that ends badly but will turn around and repeat the behavior.

The importance of the timing of attachment experiences cannot be overstated. The infant has rapid growth of brain cells in the third trimester of pregnancy and this accelerated growth continues until approximately the age of two. It is during this critical period that attachment to a primary care provider is either developed or disrupted. When attachment occurs the early period of brain growth is fostered, however, if attachment is disrupted then the child's brain growth can decelerate. Both the size and volume of the child's brain can be directly affected by early attachment experiences in addition to how the brain regions function. Nourishment can play a role in the size of the brain, but brain volume is enhanced by the interplay of positive and consistent interactions between child and primary care provider.

Healthy attachment specifically stimulates the right hemisphere of the brain. The right hemisphere matures rapidly from attachment experiences and develops well before the left hemisphere. Specifically, the right frontal region of the brain is most critical to attachment and this region's growth develops simultaneously with stimulated neural maps due to bonding experiences (Trevarthen, 1998). Attachment is so critical to the developing individual that attachment stimulated development of the orbitofrontal cortex directly impacts: social adjustment, mood regulation, personal drive, responsibility, and can have a major impact on the developing personality (Cavada & Schultz, 2000). The quality of our early attachment will have a major influence on many components of our personality and who we become as teens and adults.

The critical process of early bonding begins with sensory inputs into the brain and a feedback loop with the environment. Very early experiences have major impacts on set points (established emotional dispositions) and perceptual models within the child's brain. When something is needed or wanted, the child lets the environment know by sounding a loud and jarring vocal alarm. The care provider, usually the mother, either responds to the child in a manner to address the need, or ignores the need and intensifies the child's stress. When the care provider's response reflects attunement and comfort, the child's brain releases chemical messengers (usually dopamine, but sometimes serotonin) that reduce overall stress and the result is pleasure. When the care provider ignores the child's alarm, the brain's limbic region can perceive the situation as dire and a threat to survival through the release of glucocorticoids such as cortisol. When this occurs the brain prepares the entire body to go into survival mode, which is in itself a complex process of neuro-transmitters and hormones that puts the child in a serious stress mode. When the interaction between child and mother is comforting, bonding occurs because the child will pursue pleasure and avoid pain and this is the fundamental process of attachment that begins as a primitive drive toward the source of the pleasure. If the interaction does not reduce the stress, or even heightens the stress, the child experiences pain on a physical, emotional and even spiritual level; then the job of the brain is to adapt to this situation over time in the only way it can and that is through an attempt to avoid further painful interactions. The result is the development of a pattern of avoidance or what we call attachment difficulties. Remember the issue of early vulnerability due to the need of the child to rely on adults for safety and all needs; if attachment is disrupted then the child will avoid all future vulnerability and relationships are synonymous with being vulnerable.

Because success or failure in the bonding process, produced by consistency of experiences for the child, is a neuro-biological process, the improvement of attachment will require change at the neuro-biological level, which will be addressed in Part III.

How Attachment Helps Brain Development

The primary method used by the brain to grow and develop is through repeated stimulation. This is referred to as use-dependent maturation. When a neuron is stimulated it not only grows in size and strength, it also develops insulation around the axon with a protein known as myelin that improves the efficiency of the electric transmissions through the cell. Stimulation also creates new communication links with other cells by synaptic interconnections. Pairs, groups and networks of neurons become connected that can now do important work for the brain and all this brain development takes place due to stimulation.

Experiences of attachment, or being close and vulnerable to another person while having important survival needs met in pleasurable ways, stimulate the brain. Attachment experiences also specifically foster growth in important brain regions such as the corpus callosum (enabling communication of left and right hemispheres of the neocortex), right hemisphere (where attachment first develops), prefrontal cortex (where stress reduction and regulation develops), hippocampus (for positive intrinsic memories), limbic regions (for positive emotional states), and additional regions outlined in the next section. An understanding of how the brain develops helps in seeing the importance of repetition of experiences that repair and heal disrupted attachment. Attachment and brain development are complimentary and growth in one supports growth in the other.

Parts of the Brain Affected by Attachment

Both positive and negative influences to many brain regions can be affected by attachment. Negative impacts will primarily influence the more primitive regions of the brain's limbic system. Stimulation of the flight or fight response will impact the amygdala, the hippocampus, the anterior cingulate, and the insula. However, brain growth in these regions will be used to respond to threat rather than promote learning and exploration of the larger world. Overly developed primitive limbic regions will promote reactivity and self-protection. When these regions are stimulated and grow in importance, it inhibits growth in brain regions that will be critical to higher reasoning, such as: the left hemisphere, the right prefrontal cortex, the orbitofrontal cortex, and negative experiences slow the growth of the corpus callosum, the primary communication link between the right and left hemispheres of the brain.

Positive experiences do the opposite by promoting growth in the more complex brain regions and sending messages to the brain to rely less on primitive self-protective areas. Positive experiences better prepare the child for learning, enjoying, relaxing, and connecting and these experiences set the stage for rapid development of executive functions in the prefrontal cortex or most advanced area of the brain. The unavoidable result is that children with strong attachments growing up have brains with more developed higher reasoning centers and do better in school, do better with peers and with relationships in general. Children with insecure attachments growing up are more hesitant, reactive, self-protective in relationships, and often struggle in school.

Although the belief that distinct brain regions are solely responsible for specific brain functions, known as the localization theory, has been disproved, it is still true that areas of the brain have major roles to play in brain functioning. It is accurate to say that attachment is heavily influenced by neuro-networks in a number of brain structures such as the following:

Hypothalamus – In this area of the brain, associations are made concerning a number of factors involved in attachment. The hypothalamus is one of the earlier evolutionary regions of the brain. Although it is small, it directly impacts the nervous system and specifically the master gland of the body, the pituitary. Very early physiological processes began at birth to stimulate the hormone oxytocin that assists in childbirth, stimulating the sensitivity of the breasts and mammary glands resulting simultaneously in the production of milk, maternal instincts toward the child, and help with initial bonding with the mother through breast feeding.

Ventral Tegmental Area or VTA – This area of the brain is also an area that formed much earlier in evolution than some of the higher reasoning centers. It sits in the middle lower region of the brain and is actively involved in the brain's reward system. This small part of the brain plays a major role in desire, motivation and preferences. The primary way it does this is through the release of dopamine. The VTA has been found to be strongly involved in human pairing, intense desire for another person, and may well play an early role in the pairing between mother and child. If an early bond between child and mother is successful, the release of dopamine will stimulate desire for more connection. However, if the bond is disrupted the strong chemical bond between mother and child may not take place, resulting in impaired development of the VTA and may well influence the interest in connecting with others at each developmental period of life.

Caudate Nucleus – An area of the brain that is close to the thalamus or the gateway of sensory stimuli to the overall brain. The Caudate Nucleus has a number of roles including assisting in learning and memory. It is saturated by dopamine neurons that connect it to the Ventral Tegmental Area. The Caudate Nucleus plays a role in excitation of the brain through positive memory associations. When these roles are combined with release of the brain's pleasure drug dopamine, learning and memory connect the pleasurable early experiences of the mother and child interaction and pleasurable bonds are established in the brain. While the Caudate Nucleus is very helpful in bonding, it can also have a dark side. Later in life the Caudate Nucleus may play a role in craving and desire for pleasurable dopamine that results from sources outside the brain such as drugs, alcohol or other addictions, or mental health disorders such as obsessions and compulsions. Along with the Nucleus Accumbens Septi, the pleasure center of the primitive brain, the Caudate Nucleus can create early healthy attachment to a primary care provider or later attachments to a host of unhealthy addictions. It is, therefore, understandable that the brain that desires pleasurable stimulation from dopamine will pursue this pleasure from another source if an attachment with others is not consistently available. In this way, individuals with poor early attachment are more prone to addictions than individuals with strong early attachments.

Attachment Promotes Positive Traits

The more detailed the consideration of the impact of attachment on the brain, the more it is clear attachment is a major influence on positive brain development in many ways.

Decades of research have repeatedly found that attachment is a major influence on the developing personality of individuals. The following are only a few examples:

- Secure attachment was associated with more competent toddlers, preschoolers, and students (Belsky & Nezworkski, 1988).
- The mother's attachment with her mother predicted the attachment with her child (Lewis, et. al, 1984).
- Secure attachment increased competence with peer relationships, positive disposition, higher levels of empathy (Lewis, et. al, 1984).
- Infants with a secure attachment were more enthusiastic, persistent, and cooperative (Matos, Arend & Sroufe, 1978).

When attachment is disrupted, a number of problems have been identified in other research:

- Increased right subcortical activity predisposes the individual to negative affect, then aggressive feelings, then violent behavior (Raine, Melroy, Bihrle, Stoddard, LaCasse & Buchsbaum, 1998).
- Intense and prolonged stress can negatively impact emotional stability and the ability to trust others (Gaensbauer & Hiatt, 1983).
- Higher risk of aggression throughout life (Schore, 1994).

But the difficulties do not stop here. In the next section more detail will be provided concerning developmental difficulties due, in part, to disrupted attachments.

Impairments Associated with Lack of Attachment

Attachment is so critical to brain development and social growth that when it is lacking there can be some very serious impairments that, if not addressed in childhood, can last a lifetime. The long-term predictions for individuals with serious impairments of attachment are unhappiness, loneliness and isolated lives due, in part, to some or many of the following impairments.

Poor Socio-Emotional Information – The impact of poor attachment reduces the brain's ability to understand social encounters and the resulting emotions that take place between individuals. Impaired attachment leads to misreading the motivations of others and causes reactivity, self-protection and, at times, a fight or flight response to minor social issues. An example is when a child with disrupted attachment responds aggressively or seems compelled to run away from casual encounters with a peer or adult.

Regulation of Bodily States – The lack of attachment impairs the prefrontal cortex's ability to self-regulate and override limbic emotional and behavioral reactions to misperceived threats. Early attachment is an essential part of the development of the prefrontal cortex where perceptual and emotional bodily states are assessed and regulated. This explains the frequent over-reactivity of children with disrupted attachments. Children with insecure early attachment often act in ways that confuse or even mystify other children and adults.

Coping with Emotional Stress – When the brain and autonomic nervous system experience the stress response cycle, the result can determine if the child feels more empowered and successful in managing a stressful situation, or unsuccessful in handling stress based upon unpleasant consequences. When stress is managed in a way that the brain can turn off the glucocorticoid release in the body (which causes stress and anxiety), then the individual returns to a state of calm and the result is coded in the limbic regions of the brain as successful management of stress or what we call coping. We cope with situations that may be difficult, but we have learned we can manage them. Emotional pressure and stress are very important experiences to be able to cope with and children with attachment disruptions often fail in this area. Without the ability to cope with emotional stress, the individual is constantly at the mercy of events and circumstances in the environment and the child feels helpless and out of control, which adds to the emotional stress. This is one reason why a frequent theme of children with insecure early attachment is a strong need for control.

Understanding Sensory Information Beneath Awareness – The brain is never off duty and even in deep sleep the brain is very active. Sensory information is constantly being relayed to the brain for processing and analysis. The amount of sensory information being received by the brain is vast and the brain must be able to rapidly determine what is important to give specific attention to and what to ignore and remain background information. It is a bit like driving a car where there are dozens of moving dials on the dashboard, but most are available but not needed at any one time. It is the orbitofrontal cortex that drives the brain and makes the decisions to watch the speedometer frequently but not the temperature, electrical or gas gages unless there is a problem. The brain must be aware of thousands of sensory inputs but also must be able to determine what is important. Without this ability, which attachment helps develop in the orbitofrontal cortex, the child is overstimulated, reactive and in a constant state of overwhelming stress.

Correctly Sensing Danger – Because survival is the primary focus of the brain, it must be able to sense danger with excellent accuracy. However, disruptions of attachment can significantly reduce the brain's ability to correctly sense danger. The brain can misperceive in both directions by perceiving danger when it is not present and by missing danger that is present. Children with disrupted attachments most often perceive false positives or they sense non-existing danger. The presence of a stranger or a change in schedule can set off the fear response in the brain. The threat response can become so pervasive that the brain may become mired in perceiving one threat after another. The chronic release of adrenaline and cortisol can produce toxic stress that can profoundly impact the individual's overall health in the long run. On the other end, the child may not sense danger when it is present. He or she may ignore danger signs and perform risky behaviors. They may walk up to strangers and engage in interactions that could be risky. Because these children do not accurately sense real threat, they may become aggressive in situations where they could be easily hurt, such as provoking someone of greater size and strength and who might represent a danger. Correctly perceiving danger is a primary task of the brain and disrupted attachment impairs this essential ability. The result of this impairment is an individual who has little ability and less confidence in knowing the safe from the unsafe aspects of the world he or she experiences.

Dissociation in Young Children – The body and the brain can take only so much pain after which it switches off its sensory inputs. Therefore, the pain is still there but it is blocked from awareness. The brain process that does this is called dissociation. The process of switching off pain receptors in the brain is on the extreme end of the flight state on the fight/flight continuum. The brain knows that dissociation will make it vulnerable to threats, but it takes this drastic step when it encounters a painful situation it cannot escape from. While the process of numbing pain is a short-term adaptive step taken to protect the individual, if it continues over an extended period of time it ceases to be a healthy adaptation and becomes an impairment. The brain does not want to shut off sensory input signaling pain because it needs to monitor pain closely to insure survival.   Therefore, dissociation is an emergency step indicating how serious the brain is experiencing the pain, which is typically emotional in nature. It is important to understand how serious the brain is perceiving the pain because the job of the parent, therapist or teacher is to support the child and they must be sensitive and work to eliminate dissociation because no healing or learning can happen in a dissociative state.

Dissociation releases endogenous opioids and cortisol and the brain stem decreases blood flow and heart rate to achieve homeostasis.   One means used by the brain to create the experience of dissociation is to call upon the brain's internal pharmacy and release endogenous (internally produced) opioids with a similar chemical composition to plant-based opiates. These chemicals are analgesics, meaning they deaden pain receptors.   When the brain takes a step toward dissociation, it has already identified a state of significant threat and the pituitary or master gland of the brain has signaled the release of cortisol. To counter the discrepancy between stimulating the body and dulling the senses, the brain stem attempts to produce a state of homeostasis by restricting the excitatory response of the body—such as the heart rate, blood pressure and respiration. The 'push/pull' process in itself creates stress and contributes to a lack of congruent emotional and physical health. This is another reason why dissociation is not a consistently healthy process for any individual.

Dissociation Compared to an Animal Playing Dead – Perhaps the best analogy to human dissociation in the broader animal kingdom is how animals either play dead or go into an altered state of stasis or inactivity when they experience threats they cannot escape from. This is even found in some species of fish, such as the carp, which ceases to struggle when captured. This similarity is yet another reminder that we humans are very much a part of the animal kingdom. Like the broader animal kingdom, it is the vulnerable and less powerful species that experience this similarity to dissociation. And it is our children who are the most vulnerable and least powerful members of our human family. The power differential has also been shown when more females than males experience dissociation and more young children compared to older children, such as teens. Dissociation is associated with powerlessness, lending another explanation to the need for power and control for children with insecure attachments early in life.

Parasympathetic Activation and Going into an Inner World – Related to dissociation, the dynamic of turning off the nervous system is often an adaptation to traumatic experiences. The parasympathetic nervous system is the counterpart to the sympathetic nervous system and can be considered the 'off' switch to arousal. Without an activated nervous system, the child enters an inner world shut off from the environment all around. Children that have this experience are, at times, misdiagnosed as psychotic, but their mental and sensory systems work fine. However, the brain determines it must take a break from the stress. The best way to bring a child back is to be present with support and offer a stable environment without undue pressure, limited stress, and pleasurable stimuli. An example of such an environment would be a setting that encourages play and enjoyment.

Inter-generational Transmission of Child Abuse and Violent Behavior – Another potential outcome of the lack of attachment is the unfortunate dynamic of treating your own children the way you were treated when you were maltreated at a young age. The correlation is strong between trauma in early years and the disruption of attachment, and this increases the chances of inter-generational child abuse being handed down to yet another generation.

Disruption Now and Destruction Later

Attachment is so integral to pleasure, as well as a host of other positive states with the brain, the lack of attachment can have immediate negative consequences as well as produce long-term harm. The brain learns from experience and the newborn has limited situations to draw upon other than what has occurred the last few experiences. The newborn's brain does not yet have an effective way to consider contradictory experiences; this will develop later in the higher reasoning centers of the pre-frontal cortex. The brain also does not have an internal assessment measure other than pleasure and pain and its relationship to threats to survival. Because of this, the brain's job is to sense pain and adapt by avoiding it.

The brain initially does not make any more sophisticated judgments than pursue pleasure and avoid pain, but one thing is critical and that is to make the pleasure/pain determination quickly because the result may determine survival. An example is warmth, which is experienced by the infant as pleasurable while cold is painful. The brain knows that if there is no source of warmth then there is a very real threat to survival. The newborn must immediately test the environment in an all or nothing fundamental assessment. If the child has sensory experiences of hunger, an immediate and maximum level of alarm must be sent out and the brain carefully notices the response. With the hundreds of alarms the child sends out in a matter of hours, it does not take long for the brain to assess whether the care provider is a source of pleasure and is to be pursued to promote survival or the source of pain and must be avoided to the extent possible. For a strong bond to develop between child and mother, quick and consistent responses that satisfy needs must be initiated by the child's vocal alarms.

Since a newborn child cannot walk away or look for another source of pleasure, what the brain must do is to promote survival by accepting what can be gained by a marginal care provider and adapt to the situation as best it can. This can produce the many varying degrees of attachment bonds that have names like insecure, anxious avoidant, ambivalent, and disorganized as well as trauma bonds. Disruptions in attachment come from the child's brain adapting to far less than ideal responsiveness to the child's needs. But like a variable ratio schedule of reinforcement (such as a slot machine where you are never sure when good things will happen so you continue to try), the child reaches out not knowing the outcome and thus experiences stress each time and develops an insecure attachment. The task of the brain under such circumstances is to adapt to the extent possible.

While a wide variety of attachments or disruptions are quickly developed, there are serious long-term consequences of very early bonding experiences. It is the nature of the neuro-biological role of attachment that the instinctive feedback loop of the child and mother helps or hurts the child's ability to learn to relax and receive and internalize self-soothing. When attachment bonds are strong, the child's brain realizes it can rely on the environment (primary care provider) for safety and other basic needs. Early in life, well-attached children are more positive, more calm and well-adjusted to the people and environment around them. Reliance on the parent reduces stress and allows the brain to switch off the stress response (fight or flight) process. This is specifically accomplished within the developing right hemisphere of the brain that helps to regulate glucocorticoids, such as cortisol, and connects stress reduction with attachment (Wittling & Pfluger, 1990). However, if the child's brain learns that basic needs are poorly met or intermittently ignored, the brain must be on full alert for all basic needs or survival could be at risk. Healthy early growth in the brain helps the developing individual in some important ways such as perceptions of the environment, a sense of self, the early development of empathy, and the early stages of morality (Bigler, 2001). Brain growth in the right prefrontal cortex helps the child give meaning to visual and auditory signals from others, allowing the early development of empathy (Schore, 1994).

Over time the results of secure and insecure attachments can have major influences on the child's nervous system, disposition, personality and physical and emotional health. The early interaction of positive facial expressions from the mother (such as smiles) eliciting the same from the child, produces the child's first positive reciprocal bond. However, if the child perceives negative facial expressions, an unpleasant stress response occurs. Internal stress is experienced by the child in the same way as physical pain (Liebeskind, 1991). Early difficulties with bonding can result in generalized avoidance of social connections, particularly if the child experiences any vulnerability. The result of social avoidance can produce an individual who prefers to be alone rather than with others, to reject the enjoyment or support of others, and this can grow into a variety of anti-social personality traits or the traits of being a loner. At times, early bonding problems can result not so much in avoiding social interactions as a pattern of using others for personal gain. These are the children who will connect with others only when they get what they want and can control adults and dictate the conditions of the interaction.

A skill often underdeveloped in children with attachment problems is resiliency or the ability to handle adversity. This can be explained on a biological level in the interaction between the mother and the child. When the mother can manage her own stress and assist the child to handle the child's stress, this dynamic creates what has been called the 'rupture and repair' cycle; the child learns to recover faster as well as learning internal self-regulation, also viewed as an early indication of good mental health (Schore, 2003). The part of the mother's brain that enables her to self-regulate is the prefrontal cortex and when she soothes the child she stimulates the child's prefrontal cortex, which in turn promotes growth in this important region of the developing brain. The reciprocal feedback loop of attachment allows the parent and the child to recognize and respond to the internal states of the other and allows the amplifying of positive states and modulating negative states. The parent's ability to moderate negative affect helps organize the child's response patterns, resulting in self-regulation (Spangler, Schieche, Ilg, Maier & Ackermann, 1994).

Resiliency can be learned early through a secure attachment. However, the opposite is also true when the child experiences a feedback loop where there is a lack of attunement between mother and child. Such a pattern can be highly stressful, inducing and stimulating limbic neuro-networks rather than promoting prefrontal cortex development. When this takes place the child is anxious and reactive rather than calm and secure. The essential role that attachment plays in stress modulation and the regulation of emotions and behavior will require bonding to be an important part of repairing attachment.

Children grow to become teens and young adults with personality traits formed very early in life. As a child matures, social interactions become increasingly complex and so does the need for the child to become socially astute at reading verbal and non-verbal cues from others. At times attachment difficulties can be seen in early school experiences, but developing social problems are not always noticed in early years. Preschoolers can be temperamental, show little or no stress when separated from a parent, or little interest in being reunited at the end of the day. These children can be difficult to please or to nurture and show little concern for others. However, adults usually give considerable latitude to young children and go out of their way to teach, explain and forgive negative social displays.

By the time the child begins to interact outside the home, it is often easier to see the results of early attachment difficulties as the child struggles to keep up with the growing importance of relationships outside the family. While social requirements are often the most obvious indicators of poor early attachment, there may be many other signs. For example, elementary age children may avoid a variety of things and not just social connections. They can overreact to rules, transitions and unexpected experiences, as well as, over or underreact to pain. They may avoid learning something new because this requires them to make mistakes and experience initial failure, which they do not handle well. These children can be very controlling and difficult to please. But the most obvious signs of early difficulties with attachment have to do with social interactions.

As children with early bonding issues age, they often appear to grow physically and intellectually but not socially. This can result in the use of physical size or intellectual skill at getting what they want regardless of the impact on others. At a time that friendships become a much more important part of a child's life, these children reflect a clear lack of concern for the needs and interests of others. They may be very skilled at making friends, but they are often very poor at maintaining a friendship. As social requirements become more important and more complex, children with early attachment difficulties become more obvious and more disruptive and difficult for others to work with. Early symptoms of attachment issues can be overlooked at young ages, but the same issues are difficult to overlook as the child enters a more social world such as in school.

During the middle school or junior high school years, children with poor abilities to connect with adults or peers stand out even more than in early childhood. They may develop disciplinary problems (they like to be in control and resist the rules of others), or they may have a combination of academic and social deficiencies. A common pattern for these children is to either be a loner or to connect with other children with similar personality patterns. When two children with attachment issues relate to each other, the social deficiencies of both individuals are not a good formula for relationship success. This dynamic can play out with friendships where the children may be attracted to each other, but do poorly at maintaining a relationship. Later on this dynamic can occur with love interests, often producing poor results. As the individual enters adulthood, this same dynamic can result in failed marriages and other relationships. Therefore, early attachment deficiencies are not just a problem in childhood years.

High school years increase the level of complexity of social interactions and children with attachment problems must navigate the next complex step of social interaction, and that is to form a love interest with another person. Developing a dating or intimate relationship with a peer may be what is going on all around these young people, but to them this is contrary to their social disposition. These young people may form relationships with other peers, but it usually is entirely from self-interest. All such young people are not distasteful to interact with, some have learned skills to impress and then to manipulate. It is in the teen years that many personality disorders can develop that may last the rest of their lives. There are many examples of individuals who appear on the surface to be successful, but are unable to have a meaningful social life. Whether a child is a loner or a socially engaged manipulator, there are usually obvious signs of distress and unhappiness. It is connection with people that will provide what these children lack and no amount of control, influence or material accumulation can fill the social void they feel. It is also through connection and relationships that we learn to manage our stress, and the years leading up to adulthood can be the most stressful period of life.

Early adulthood brings on a host of new challenges that young people with bonding problems are not prepared to successfully address. At a time when many peers are becoming serious about a romantic relationship, young adults with attachment problems for the most part have only been able to start relationships but not foster them. The advantages of being young and independent with no burdensome attachments, now begins to be out of step with others the same age. These young adults are looking for a good time, looking for physical pleasure, and do not understand why it is not the same with the other person in their short-term liaisons. Often charismatic in many ways, these young people may attract friends or lovers but leave a path of disappointment in failed relationships of a romantic or close friendship nature. Without the comfort of fulfilling human connection, these young adults often look for sensory enjoyment from more predictable sources such as alcohol and drugs. The predictable impact of stress release from drugs and alcohol can become significantly more important at this developmental period of life.

It is not just in close friendships and romantic relationships that these young people fail, they also have difficulty in most other socially demanding parts of living such as employment. These young adults tend not to be team players; they take what is offered and give little back. They are not ideal employees except for a few professions such as sales and other competitive environments such as some business enterprises and politics. There are frequent reports of deceit and using others among competitive businesses and politics. Failures in social aspects of living throughout their childhood, teen years and now young adult period often leaves an emptiness of spirit that is temporarily masked by various addictions but is not ameliorated. The high of a substance cannot take the place of love and support from others. As the years go by, these young adults can get further away from the connections that are the source of contentment and enjoyment that humans need.

There is another learning opportunity for some young adults with poor early attachments who return to the vulnerable area of social interest. For these young people, there is an inner drive to get close to others that requires levels of vulnerability, yet an internal conflict arises due to an approach/avoidance conflict. They may now feel a need to do precisely what they have evaded most of their lives. Just pursuing connection with others may be a healthy step in the right direction, but interest alone does not make up for many years of undeveloped social skills such as empathy. However, interest in connection with others can go a long way to give the young person a fighting chance at a less isolated and lonely life. Young adults with significant attachment deficits often marry and just as often divorce. They may be very skilled at producing a child but not successfully caring for and parenting a child. The resulting impact on the child of a distant parent can repeat the pattern into the next generation. Disrupted marriages and relationships happen with both the uninterested and unattached young adults as well as the new converts to connection who cannot manage the challenges of relying on another person.

Adult years bring the final challenges for individuals with early attachment problems. With or without families and friendships, these adults lack the social ingredients of contentment and happiness — such as having people they can trust and rely on, loving and being loved, and a deep connection to something greater than oneself. Now the individual has lived a life of struggle without the safe haven of love and connection. They have as many challenges in life, if not more, than attached individuals, but they lack the greatest source of stress relief — loving connection to others. They have found momentary comfort in alcohol, drugs and perhaps temporary connection through physical sex, but they have not found a place to rest and let down their guard. A life of responding to stress with a fight or flight response has produced a significant amount of stress hormones. Stress hormones such as cortisol, epinephrine, and adrenalin are functional and healthy in the short-term, but if the stress response cycle is activated often then the result is anything but healthy. Chronic activation of stress hormones kills healthy cells, particularly neurons, and over many years the body's ability to heal and fight back from illness can be compromised.

There have been anecdotal reports for hundreds of years that humans in the face of unbearable stress can lose consciousness and even die. There have been incidents in war zones and prisoner of war camps where physically healthy men get to the point of completely giving up and this can lead to the expression "losing heart" and the result can be death by cardiomyopathy, a condition that mimics a heart attack and is literally a broken heart (Wittstein, Thiemann, Lima, Baughman, Schulman, Gerstenblith, Wu, Rade, Vivalacqua & Champion,

2005). After years of such reports, there is now ample scientific evidence that particularly chronic release of stress hormones can cause the breakdown of systems of the body, in particular the auto-immune system and can result in a variety of medical diseases (Felitti, Anda, et. al, 1998). Therefore the emotional and ultimately physical price of a lack of attachment is a child who is isolated and unhappy and reactive. The older child is stressed and has poor relationships, teens begin to look for the antidote to loneliness and emptiness, moving into young adulthood alone and unhappy. Finally, with decades of chronic stress comes the breakdown of the body's ability to recover and the result can be the major medical diseases that can ruin later years of life and significantly shorten the individual's lifespan. Therefore, children who do not learn to bond and attach not only are more prone to unhappy lives, but are also likely to die much younger than their attached peers. Because of the poor physical health prognosis for individuals with poor attachments, it is fair to call attachment problems not only a recipe for an unhappy life but also a silent killer.

Attachment and Social Success

When all real success is social success, then early attachment becomes the means to a life that is fulfilled, happy and successful. Research on happiness has produced clear patterns of what does and does not promote contentment in life. Happiness is not related to youth, wealth, education, notoriety, or power and influence although many of these attributes are desirable to our western appetites. Happiness is directly related to social support, close relationships, engagement in life and most directly correlated to a sense of meaning and purpose, such as helping others. Strong, healthy relationships are the most direct route to a full and satisfying life. For this reason, attachment is critically important. There are many ways that attachment will facilitate social success and some of the most important are the following.

Self-Understanding – We spend much of our lives, particularly in the early years, working on self-understanding. It may be that we never complete this process since each developmental level in life brings up new aspects of who we are. Self-understanding goes beyond the discovery of our thoughts and emotions related to people and experiences of living, it needs to become an experience of continuity that before and after influential experiences we are the same person. The individual needs the experience of coherence or the result will be confusion and a fractured identity. Attachment plays a key role in the development of self-understanding as well as the experience of self-coherence. We learn who we are in relation to others and it is in social situations that most individuals best grow in knowledge of self, including one's personality. Without meaningful attachments throughout life, the self will most likely be unrealized and the lack of understanding oneself can be yet another source of internal stress.

Positive Neurodevelopment – Attachment promotes and facilitates brain growth. Positive attachment experiences will stimulate the precise regions of the brain that will come to be critical to contentment and happiness. The higher reasoning centers of the left and right prefrontal cortex, as well as the orbitofrontal cortex, are involved in positive attachments and will become the regions of the brain that are most critical to the personality. But they go far beyond influencing personality, they also are the centers of thoughtful consideration, conceptual analysis, abstract thought, as well as, the dozens of executive functions of the brain including: delaying gratification, planning, learning from the past, setting goals, and mental flexibility to name just a few. The brain develops from the more primitive to the more complex regions and attachment

71

promotes growth in the brain's most complex areas. Later social success will rely heavily on the capacity of the higher reasoning centers and in this way social success and attachment are inseparable.

Perceptual Clarity of Social Cues – A very complex aspect of social interaction is to correctly perceive the messages and intentions of others. It is very common that children with poor early attachments are severely delayed in understanding social complexity. The brain must correctly perceive any threat in order to promote survival and any mistake will be on the side of seeing a threat even if none exists. Attachment is a great help to children in attuning to others and aligning emotions with first the mother and then others throughout life. Early attachment disruption can cause over-reactivity to situations with little or no element of threat. This dynamic can cause these children and later adults to misperceive the intentions and motivations of others. Trust requires vulnerability, which is problematic if the individual expects a negative outcome based upon the perceived ill intent of the other person. Early attachment sets the stage for success or failure in being vulnerable. The fact that the infant's brain rapidly adapts to disruptions of attachment may well develop a personality unwilling and even unable to be vulnerable.

Acceptance of Support – One of the prime antidotes to stress is the social support of others. The brain very early in life experiences 'rescue and recovery' from a solid attachment with a primary care provider. To the infant, any number of daily experiences provide a source of threat and therefore stress. Being hungry, cold, ill, tired, lonely, wet, thirsty, and a host of other experiences are initially all perceived as threats by the early development of the primitive limbic region of the brain. The child cannot meet personal needs without signaling an alarm and receiving the nurturance needed. When the child cries due to hunger and is not only fed but provided warm nurturing touch, then the neuro-pathways of attachment develop that will thereafter link needs with reaching out for the support and help of others. With a disrupted bond, the child does not receive the rescue and therefore does not recover from the stress and chronic or toxic stress can develop. Far worse than this, the brain learns that reaching out to other is not only unsuccessful but it is painful and must be avoided. Adults who are unable to accept the support and help of others have more stress, more medical problems, more depression, higher rates of self-harm, higher rates of substance abuse and as a group they do not live as long as adults who have social support. The determining experiences for accepting the support of others take place very early in life, much before there is conscious awareness of a developing pattern.

Empathy – This is the ability to accurately understand the experience and emotions of another person. The preconditions of empathetic understanding are receiving empathy or being on the receiving end of a connection with another person who is interested and understands. Without this experience, it is unlikely that a full capacity to be empathetic will develop. It is difficult to imagine a successful relationship of any kind that does not include empathetic understanding on both ends. Children feel badly when a peer falls off a bicycle, and very young children may say, "Is mommy sad?" when they see tears. Empathy begins early in life with the attachment to a care provider. Responsiveness produces a reciprocal interaction between mother and child, and from this foundation early stages of empathy transfer to others. One of the most pervasive deficiencies of children with bonding disruptions is the lack of an interest or capacity to empathize with others.

Interdependence with Others - Few emotionally healthy people wish to be dependent upon another person for any extended period of time. When we are young children dependence is necessary, but even then the optimal mother/child relationship has some component of both individuals dependent upon the other. To feel dependent is the ultimate vulnerability, which need not be a negative experience if the results are successful. Early attachment could be said to be a successful experience of dependency, and vulnerability may not be perceived by the developing brain as a threat to survival. Optimum relationship, or healthy attachments, are interdependent in that the vulnerability and success of needs being met go both directions. The early attachment is the precursor to friendships and intimacy later in life. Disrupted attachment is the beginning of suspicion, distancing and disrupted connections with others, possibly throughout life.

Coping – This is the ability to manage the stress of life that inevitably challenges everyone. The ability to cope allows the individual to face the stress and not be overcome or damaged by it. Coping includes the ability to be resilient or being able to bounce back from adversity. Coping is directly related to early experiences of managing stress. Since the infant has very limited ability to handle stress, the quality of attachment will have much to say about the coping ability of the child. With a secure attachment the child learns that everyday stress can be managed through the alarm, rescue and repair cycle of bonding. The human brain is less focused on the significance of the stress than past experience at surviving the stress. When the infant repeatedly survives stress through the support and nurturance of the mother, the brain responds with the recovery process referred to as coping. Therefore, coping is yet another critical element of later success that is dependent upon early attachment.

Positive Affective Disposition - The importance of positive affect has received increased attention, particularly from the research in positive psychology. A great many advantages come to individuals who have primarily positive emotions about their experiences and their lives. Positive emotions promote physical as well as emotional health; they help with managing stress, resiliency, number and quality of close relationships and overall happiness (Kubzansky, Sparrow, Vokonas & Kawachi, 2001). People who have mainly positive affect not only have better lives, but they also have longer lives. A major influence over the emotional state of an individual is early attachment to a primary care provider. Children who experience the safety and comfort of a responsive parent begin life with the experience of positive emotions and this can become the habitual pattern or what John Bowlby in Attachment Theory called the individual's set-point for emotional expression (Bowlby, 1982). It is simplistic but generally accurate that early attachment produces positive emotions that become a positive affective disposition throughout life.

Moral and Ethical Reasoning – In a somewhat less direct way than positive emotions, attachment promotes moral and ethical reasoning. Early attachment encourages a sensitivity to others and thus a social orientation. Moral reasoning requires that the individual move beyond egocentricity and narcissism where other people are means to an end and are there to be used and often abused. When a child has poor early bonding experiences, the brain develops around self-centered concerns such as safety. If early social experiences do not meet the individual's needs, then the brain must maintain the primary self-focus. Only when successful bonding occurs does the brain see the value in connecting, initiating, and taking the emotional state of others into consideration and developing a sense of empathy. From empathy the prefrontal cortex can develop the concepts of right and wrong or moral reasoning and a developing conscience. Ethical reasoning is related to morality, but could be viewed as the highest step in that ethical decisions are the highest level of moral reasoning in Kohlberg's scale. At this stage of moral reasoning, the individual has a sense of universal justice and fairness for its own sake (Kohlberg, Levine & Hewer, 1983). Once again, attachment is a primary building block of moral and ethical reasoning.

To summarize the biological processes at work with attachment, early bonds will start a cycle of successful connections with a primary care provider, then a larger circle of social contacts, later friends, then intimate partners, and then the cycle repeats itself with bonding with the individual's own children. However, the opposite is also clear that early disruption of the bonding process produces increased stress, mood dysregulation and rough childhood years, often leading to peer conflicts, social isolation, poorly developed relationships on all levels and growing social failure. These two paths can make the difference between a happy and fulfilled life and a life of anxiety and unhappiness leading to a host of social and even medical difficulties.

Certainly no good parent and no healthy community or society would want a child to begin life with the disadvantages of poor attachment in early years. The most efficient way to address this problem is to encourage bonding between parent and child. Many preventive efforts have been used in the last few decades, including parenting classes, neonatal parental support, public health campaigns encouraging prenatal care, and even efforts such as reducing domestic violence and reducing poverty. But preventive efforts will not help the child who has already experienced the damage of poor early attachment. For these children we must take what we have learned about the process of attachment and repair the damage as early as possible.

Part III: Attachment Problems – How to Repair and Improve Attachment

If you have started reading this book in this section, you likely are working with a child with attachment problems, and you want to know what to do about it now, not later. If so, this is understandable and it will work just fine to begin the book here. However, it is suggested that after finishing Part III that you return to the previous two sections because what you will read here will make sense in a deeper way with the previous information. If you have started at the beginning, you have been patient, and it is now time to make it worth your while by going into specifics as to how to improve attachment in children for whom this does not come easy.

Don't be fooled into believing that repairing attachment is too complicated for you to be successful. Also don't be surprised to find out that some of the best ways to repair attachment are quite simple and straightforward. However, a straightforward solution does not mean an easy solution. For example, on a recent trip to France I learned the motto of the French people – "Liberté, Egalité, Fraternité" or "Freedom, Equality and Brotherhood." While this noble motto is straightforward, it is anything but easy to achieve in practice. Repairing attachment is much the same. What you want to accomplish is clear, and how to get there is also easy to understand; however, the journey is long, and it is usually a bumpy ride.

The theme of this section is a practical guide to repairing attachment. The most practical of principles is that knowing what went wrong early in life informs what needs to be repaired. Whatever initially harmed the child must be healed, and whatever the child missed must now be provided. Any adult who would like to help repair attachment must become an attachment figure for the individual who is being helped.

When it comes to children, it is essential to understand that the child will likely resist any and all efforts to help. They speak in opposites, they will tell you to go away, and they don't want what you are selling. These children are not happy with their situation, but they will do everything in their power to avoid vulnerability or the possibility of further pain and disappointment. They will also act in ways contrary to what is best for them. This comes from the part of the child's brain that does much of the mental processing—the limbic region. It is this part of the brain that controls emotions, threat response and intrinsic memories of past pain. This combination places the child in a reactive stance and impairs the ability to use higher reasoning centers to understand what are good decisions or what would be helpful to them. Avoiding genuine emotions, staying far away from close connection with others, and achieving a power position to have as much control over others and situations as possible are the primary goals of children with insecure attachments. These are the dynamics that must be reversed. To help provide clear suggestions, recommended interventions and tips in this section will be highlighted as shown here.

> ▶ Although the causes and brain mechanisms of attachment disruption have been shown in earlier sections to be considerably complex, such complexity need not point to a discouraging prognosis. Do provide for the child what he or she missed by not having a nurturing biological parent. Don't listen to the empty words of protest because children often say the opposite of what they really mean.

Because attachment is so closely linked to the dynamics of the brain, by its nature it is very complex. In the previous two sections the roots of attachment disruption have been covered and how attachment, or lack of, develops within the brain and then becomes a major sculpting force for brain development over time. It is easy to see how some have viewed problems with attachment as too difficult to repair and to consider attachment recovery so complex as to be impossible. However, many aspects of brain repair possible today were viewed as impossible in the recent past. Brain repair is what improving attachment essentially does. If we can identify what went wrong and how it went wrong, then we should have helpful information as to what we need to do to repair insecure or absent attachments.

In Part I the process of attachment has been considered in traditional behavioral terms as well as adding affective, physical, inter-personal and spiritual states of connectedness. The goal thus far has been to describe how, when, and why attachment or the lack of attachment occurs. Part II explained in neuro-biological terms how the brain adapts and develops in part dependent upon the quality of attachment early in life. The focus now turns to a discussion of assessment and moves to briefly covering multiple issues that will be encountered in the repair process of attachment problems. Brain informed approaches to improve attachment will be discussed--including a detailed model for treating attachment disturbances that has been tested over the last three decades with good success in working with very serious attachment disruptions in young children.

Attachment theory was previously explained to form the foundation for attachment interventions. For all its strengths, the question that remains not fully answered in traditional attachment theory is what can be done to repair attachment problems. This is not to downplay the contribution attachment theory has made, but it provides few, if any, answers or prescriptions for the problems. Attachment theory also does not attempt to answer whether attachment can be developed later in life when no attachment develops in the first months and years of a child's life. The volume of cases where attachment disruptions are primary concerns has required the therapy world and adoption workers and families to ask these and many other important questions. Attachment theory during most of its existence has lacked the insight provided by sophisticated brain research. With new information on brain functioning and development, finding the answers to questions about attachment repair has required clinicians and parents to forge new ground and go beyond attachment theory.

The use of the term disorder comes from the diagnosis Reactive Attachment Disorder in the Diagnostic and Statistical Manual of Mental Disorders (American Psychiatric Association, 2013). The term disorder requires an explanation. The presence of a Reactive Attachment Disorder in a child in most cases indicates dysfunction in the child's initial parent, not the child. The behaviors associated with this diagnosis are inherently adaptive and functional in the child's initial situation. It made survival sense to the developing brain to avoid the cause of pain and threat, and this meant avoiding contact with unsupportive adults. Disturbances of attachment were caused by the child's environment, mainly the primary care provider(s). Because of this, the repair process must principally be based on the total environment, not solely on the child.

> ▶ The best attachment interventions address the total environment-- where all influences encourage the child to connect, needs are being consistently met, and the brain experiences the benefits of relying on others.

James has identified the roots of attachment in fundamental interactions such as: crying/responding, proximity seeking, attention getting and distress/comfort. She goes on to set out the progressive mission of attachment—first, protection of the child, second, providing for the many needs of the child, and third, guiding the child in understanding and maneuvering in social interaction (James, 1994). A number of factors can disrupt each of these social transmissions, but few as massively as the trauma resulting from child abuse. One of the most damaging dimensions of abuse is the frequency that the abuser is a primary care provider. Statistically, the most frequent source of abuse when all types of maltreatment are considered is the child's biological mother. The mission of attachment can be immediately thwarted in these cases when the child experiences neither protection nor being provided with basic needs. It may not take long before the child's proximity seeking and signaling of distress become the avoidance and manipulative control so often seen in children with trauma caused attachment disruptions.

Assessing the Extent of Damaged Attachment

Before the focus turns to solutions, it is important to determine the type, nature and the extent of the attachment problems. A variety of methods have been used to assess attachment disruptions, including the often used "Strange Situation" described in Part I. Observational areas have been used by clinicians to examine the mother/child bond, including: 1) intensity of conflict, 2) duration of disturbance, 3) generalizability of dysfunction, 4) level of dysfunction in learning capacity, 5) existence of oppositional behavior, 6) negativism in response to requests, 7) passivity in interaction, 8) overly compliant behavior, and 9) ineffectiveness and lack of persistence in problem-solving behavior (James, 1994). James goes on to say the following:

> The evaluator must assess the quality and nature of the child's trauma-related interaction patterns in order to adequately and accurately assess the quality and nature of a traumatized child's attachment behavior patterns...a partial set of questions that reflect these subtle but important distinctions include

at least the following: Under what conditions is the child compliant? Who regulates the intensity of feelings in the interaction between adult and child? Does the adult help the child function more independently or dependently? How does the adult achieve this support? To what extent are the boundaries between adult behavior and child behavior maintained or blurred? How are these boundaries established? Under what condition does the child engage in exploration? Does the child use the adult to enhance his or her ability to explore? Does the adult take over and dictate what the child should do? To what extent does the adult coach the child regarding possible solutions to problems? If the child has a high activity level, under what observable conditions does this activity level change? Does the child's behavior regress during interactions with the adult? If so, in what ways is this regression observable? Is the regression appropriate to the situation? Does the child show anxiety when the adult must leave the room? If so, how? What is the child's response to the adult's return? (James, 1994).

A variety of instruments and clinical methods have been developed to assist in the assessment of attachment disturbance, including this author's Attachment Disorder Assessment Scale - Revised (Ziegler, 2004). Assessing attachment can be challenging, time consuming and expensive. The Strange Situation is primarily a research intervention. However, I developed the ADAS-R to be quick, reliable, inexpensive and practically useful. Some assessment methods use observations of the child and mother, and some like the ADAS-R rely on information provided by someone who knows the child well, perhaps in addition to other clinical assessment instruments. Whatever methods the assessing clinician uses, attachment is so important to the developing child that a wise evaluator will consider attachment within any comprehensive assessment of a child. This was rarely done in the past, but it is gaining recognition as a critically important aspect of a psychological and mental health assessment of a child.

> ▶ How can you tell the extent of the attachment problems with the child you are working with? A full assessment of attachment can be complicated, but one answer is the quick, easy and reliable tool called the Attachment Disorder Assessment Scale – Revised. In 15 minutes it will assess the extent of the problem and make suggestions for the next step.

A brief comment must be made at this point concerning a topic that is complex and needs more discussion than will be provided here—the trauma bond. Some behaviors that appear to be signs of attachment in children are actually seriously confused interactions which are the opposite of healthy attachment. These attachment-like behaviors have been called trauma bonds and have as their purpose self-protection by giving special attention to an abusive parent by the child. These displays of interest, loyalty and extreme compliance are bred out of fear and concern for survival on the part of the child. It is essential to distinguish between healthy attachment and a trauma bond because, to the untrained eye, they may look similar. One of the best ways to distinguish the two is if the attachment produces a reduction of stress in the child rather than increasing stress.

Repairing Attachment

To identify clinical solutions, we must first identify specific problems that develop from disrupted attachment. The following quote from Herman effectively starts this discussion:

> The child trapped in an abusive environment is faced with formidable tasks of adaptation. She must find a way to preserve a sense of trust in people who are untrustworthy, safety in a situation that is unsafe, control in a situation that is terrifyingly unpredictable, power in a situation of helplessness. Unable to care for or protect herself, she must compensate for the failures of adult care and protection with the only means at her disposal, an immature system of psychological defenses (Herman, 1992).

One important point mentioned in the above is the adaptation of the child. To a large extent, most attachment disruptions are adaptations to initially unresponsive, painful, or in some way unsuccessful attempts to attach. A serious challenge arises when the child's adaptations become psychologically ingrained. When this occurs, the child is neither aware that they have made the adaptation, nor do they remember why they are acting the way they are. Nearly all attachment adaptations are pre-cognitive, meaning the individual cannot recall the causal events due to the age of onset of the developing pre-verbal brain. For this reason, the deepest levels of attachment issues are not available to insight or cognitive interventions. Because attachment issues seldom improve with standard mental health therapies, an understandable but incorrect assumption is made that the problem cannot be treated.

> ► Don't expect the child to have insight or self-awareness about bonding problems. You must create the repair plan and implement it regardless of the response of the child, since the child does not see the problem nor a need to make any changes.

James has identified a number of other outcomes of poor attachment that may need to be addressed in repairing attachment and bonding:

- When a child adapts by playing a role for the parent, the child loses themselves in the role and has no sense of self.
- Actual or perceived trauma overwhelms the child's ability to cope with life.
- Regressed or even infantile behavior is common.
- Other issues include hypervigilance, heightened startle response, irritability, anxiety, hyperactivity and dissociation.
- Numbing and avoidance of affect are frequent.
- The alarm/numbing response produces arousal in the form of anxiety from the trauma and then numbing when the anxiety gets extreme.
- Understanding risks and the ability to problem solve are often poorly developed skills.
- The exploring and learning process is halted, and the focus turns to safety, as well as needs and wants.
- Attachment problems may incorrectly be viewed as hyperactivity, low IQ, oppositional defiance, or conduct disorder (James, 1994).

The list above is only the beginning of the concerns that face adults working with these children. There is evidence that physiological systems of the child are being negatively influenced by the disruption of attachment. The child's brain may learn to organize around a stress response at a very early age (James, 1994). The trauma arousal may even be neurologically addictive by activating production of endogenous opioids, which mask signals from pain receptors thus alleviating pain and stress and may then intensify the trauma bond (van der Kolk, 1989). The unhealthy trauma bond becomes reinforced neurologically, and the child's attention and loyalty to the abuser becomes stronger as they view their survival in the hands of the source of threat—the abusive parent. In this bizarre world, the child may learn to survive by developing a level of closeness (a trauma bond) with the abusive parent, but they also learn that intimacy is to be avoided at all costs. The unavoidable results are degrees of symptoms such as: ego deficiency, handicapped emotional relationships, connections with others based on needs, lack of emotional claim to a care provider, impaired intellectual functioning, deficiency to regulate aggressive impulses as well as frustration and displeasure (Bates and Bayles, 1988).

> ► Chronic stress and anxiety in these children can be addressed by teaching the child to slow down and relax by any number of methods, such as deep breathing, periods of calm play, and quiet reading. The child may complain, but you are providing an essential skill the child will need—reducing the stress response cycle.

Several other factors of disrupted attachment deserve at least brief mention. Parenting styles require attention in cases where attachment is an issue. In a study of parental discipline styles abused children had more problem behaviors and more oppositional responses to parents. Abusive parents were more punitive in discipline, more angry when disciplining and punishment was not altered to fit the situation (Trickett and Kuczynski, 1985). Social support for single parent mothers may be another important intervention. In a study of neglectful mothers, they reported less social support and people in their environment viewed them as deviant and not wanting support (Polansky, Gaudin, Ammons & Davis, 1985). The role of the parent was pivotal in a study of one-year-olds who showed more positive and less negative affect with happy signaling from the parent (Hershberg and Svejda, 1990).

> ▶ Avoid the temptation to use any form of punishment despite all the poor decisions and behavioral problems displayed. Use logical consequences instead and help the child see the cause and effect of decisions and behaviors. All forms of punishment produce distancing between parent and child, which is the opposite of repairing attachment.

Three important areas where attachment must be remediated are: 1) the development of a social rather than anti-social personality, 2) the regaining of childhood, and 3) the growth of a conscience. Much of what has been discussed refers to a social or anti-social orientation. The process of survival, pleasing the parent, and constantly adapting to a harsh and unsafe environment will rob the child of his or her childhood. Successful intervention requires giving the child a chance to once again have childhood experiences and to return to them their childlikeness.

> ▶ Play is critical to a healthy child and forms the foundation of childhood. Many children with attachment problems do not engage in childlike play. All effective plans to promote healing and the repair of attachment teach and promote play. A further discussion of the importance of childlike play can be found at http://www.jaspermountain.org/childlike_play_traumatic_experience .pdf

A child with a disrupted attachment will often have a poorly developed conscience. To develop a conscience the child must experience connectedness to others, which gives an ability to read other's emotions and react with pleasure based upon the joy of others or distress to the signals of distress in others. The child then learns to attune first with the parent and then to others, thus planting the seeds of a conscience (Kochonska, 1993). The parent plays an important role in conscience development, including discipline without an emphasis on power, thus appealing to a child's internal sense of wrongdoing. This results in more internalization and a developing conscience (Kochonska, 1991). Whether developing a social orientation comes first or a conscience comes first is less relevant than the essential need for both to develop.

> ▶ The lack of moral reasoning in a child can be concerning to adults. Moral development takes a long time, and it is helped by improved attachment with an adult. Avoid moral lectures or moral criticism until you have a better bond with the child. For example, if a child is not truthful, then point out the importance to you of getting accurate information rather than the lack of morality in the "lie."

Factors That Influence Reattachment

There is no single scenario that the majority of attachment problems fit into, but several that deserve discussion. Regardless of the situation, the goal in clinical attachment work is to facilitate the reciprocal, enduring affiliation between parent and child if this is possible. However, there are factors to be considered that may stand in the way of attachment. This does not mean that attachment interventions should not be initiated, but it does mean that we must recognize the stress factors and inhibitors in the child's life that are potentially working against the clinical goal.

The first factor is the attachment history of the child. In most cases, there are understandable and often logical reasons why attachment problems initially develop. In general, attachment problems are adaptations on the part of the child for survival and self-protection. It means little to the child who has distancing and avoidance behaviors that the threat, the abuse, and the pain of the past are long gone. For children who have a brain that remembers the pain and vulnerability, it is like it happened yesterday. For children too young to consciously remember, their bodies, through neurological processes that store trauma memories independently, do the remembering for them (van der Kolk, 1989). The child may be fortunate to start fresh in a loving and supportive environment, but traumatized children can never start totally fresh, their past is always with them. Without understanding their past, the clinician or parent cannot hope to understand the child's present. Because of the child's past experiences, perceptions develop that fit their working models of themselves and others. Until adults understand this, they cannot fully know the child.

Trauma bonds have been briefly discussed. One of the best diagnostic indicators of a trauma bond is an intense loyalty to the abusive or neglectful parent. It appears at times that the strength of the loyalty is in direct proportion to the seriousness of the neglect and/or abuse. Loyalty is also one of the outgrowths of loss, which is a significant and complex topic in itself. To many children, loss of the primary parent, regardless of the reason, is the loss of love, safety and protection (James, 1994). Where loyalty comes into play very directly is when the child perceives that any attachment, particularly if it is positive, will be a direct betrayal of the loyalty they feel for the abuser. Understanding why they feel loyal often needs no more justification to the child than because it is their "real mother" or "real father." Unless the child has never experienced any form of attachment, which is rare, loyalty should be a consideration in working with the child.

Other potentially influencing factors in a mother/child attachment are physical and/or psychiatric conditions with either the child or parent. A child cannot be accurately diagnosed with an attachment disorder if they are currently being abused. This must be one of the first investigative inquiries. Various psychiatric conditions with either the parent or child can substantially affect attachment. Issues such as addiction of the parent, dissociation, schizophrenia, mood disorders, and parental developmental delays, or even a low intelligence level on the part of a parent can create barriers and make the parent physically or emotionally unavailable. The same result can come from the presence of these same psychiatric factors in the child. If the child perceives, correctly or incorrectly, that they are likely to lose the parent to illness, they may opt to withdraw and protect themselves. This can be a major hidden factor with children who have lost a primary attachment due to illness, suicide or even death by accidental means.

The complexity of attachment work can seem overwhelming. Already in Part III many important issues to consider have been mentioned. It is now time to outline a treatment process for attachment disorder therapy. James makes several general points that are useful when considering the repair process: 1) the professional help of individual therapy is inadequate to treat attachment problems alone, 2) the environment must become a treatment milieu, 3) addressing the child's past history must come when a relationship has been developed, 4) children should not be forced to explore their trauma or loss, 5) young children should not be asked to say good-bye to a loss without having something to take its place, 6) provide support, hope and guidance, 7) follow the child's pace with accepting a loss and 8) provide a nurturing environment where a relationship of safety, consistency and emotional closeness is possible (James, 1994).

James identifies five steps in the repair of attachment difficulties: a) teaching, b) self-identity work, c) affect modulation, d) relationship building, and e) mastering behavior (James, 1994).

A Model for Treating Attachment Disturbances

The model that will now be outlined is a general description of the components that need to be present for attachment to be repaired. This model is an attempt to combine in practical application many of the components discussed thus far. After discussing this model, specific and more detailed aspects of attachment repair will be covered.

I receive my share of unusual communication from a variety of sources, and a number of years ago I received a call from someone I did not know who opened the conversation by issuing a challenge. He explained that he was the chairman of a counseling department at a university, and he said his understanding was that I claimed to do therapy to heal attachments. He was clear he did not believe in such therapy and asked me to explain to him just how I accomplished this seemingly unattainable goal. I actually enjoy to be challenged or I might have politely said I was too busy at the moment to spar with him on this complex topic. I accepted the challenge. At that point I had been working to repair attachments for many years, but I had not previously documented what I told the professor. I listed the components in this way: 1) The starting place is the child must be in a safe setting where the child experiences safety or the child's brain will perceive a threat and work against the goal of connecting with other, 2) The child in treatment must have his or her needs unconditionally met or further threats to basic needs will create a negative reactive response, 3) Consistent invitations to connection must be extended by the adults in the environment regardless of how hard the child pushes everyone away, and 4) A reciprocal environment must be created to connect the child's many wants (not needs) to something the child gives in return, creating the experience of a positive give and take of connection and relationship. When I concluded my four ingredients of repairing attachment, there was silence on the phone and the professor finally said, yes I see this could work, and he thanked me for my time. I never heard anything further from the professor but I should have thanked him because the phone call gave me an excellent chance to succinctly lay out the ingredients of repairing attachment. There is more detail I have added over the years, but the four main points remain the same.

1. The starting place is the child must be in a safe setting where the child experiences safety or the child's brain will perceive a threat and work against the goal. It should be very clear by now that safety is a precondition for healing and repairing attachment. Since attachment is all about the brain, it is actually not safety that is important but the experience and perception of safety by the child. There are situations in which children are not safe but they think they are. For example, some children in war zones can be relatively unaffected because they adjust to the conditions, and they do not perceive how unsafe they are. More often children are safe but perceive that they are not. The important point is that the child must experience and perceive a genuine condition of safety.

2. The child must have his or her needs unconditionally met or further threats to basic needs will create a negative reactive response. A common approach by adults to train children in desired behaviors and expressions of feelings is to give or withhold approval. For most children this can be one of the most effective forms of shaping a child's behavior because most children want approval, and they want to please the care provider. However children with disrupted attachments perceive that withholding approval is withholding a basic need. Therefore, for these children all basic needs must be met without conditions. A good parent would not withhold food or water due to a child's misbehavior. It is important to consider

that other basic needs must be provided without conditions, such as clothing, physical touch and love. Parents cannot withhold any basic need without the brains of these children sensing a threat--that if one need is conditional then all basic needs could become conditional.

3. Consistent invitations to connection must be extended by the adults in the environment regardless of how hard the child pushes everyone away. In many ways this third step of the process is the most challenging. Children with disrupted attachments are often very skilled at pushing adults away as well as being someone others would like to avoid. All manner of unpleasantness is fair game for these children. They learn what repulses people, and that is what they gravitate to. Bodily functions, toileting issues, sexual talk and behavior, unbridled selfishness, lying, aggression, spitting on someone and a very long list of other just as unpleasant behaviors are all ways they keep others away, thinking it is for self-protection. This step requires that the adults not give the child the power to have repulsive behavior succeed at distancing others. If the child is successful in pushing people away then everyone loses. Therefore, the adults must continue to not only issue invitations to connect, but the adults must sincerely want closeness with the child. Again, in some ways this is the most difficult of the four conditions of attachment repair and requires persistence and endurance from a caring adult.

4. A reciprocal environment must be created to connect the child's many wants (not needs) to something the child gives in return, creating the experience of the positive give and take of connection and relationship. Although this step demands hard work and creativity, it is not as difficult as step three because most adults can relate to demanding a give and take in the relationship particularly since they have received so little from the child. The challenge is to avoid having basic needs

conditional, but instead to insure that the child's many wants are very conditional upon some effort and response on the part of the child. Most adults believe it is their job to give the child what the child wants because parenting is all about giving. This is a misunderstanding of what good parenting is and can quickly become a major problem for the constant demands of children with insecure attachments. Parenting is about giving, but the type of giving makes a difference. As children mature and are given everything they desire without the expectation of giving back (reciprocation), the child can become monstrously unbearable to be around. This is actually the worst type of parenting because it gives the child the message that total selfishness will allow the child to have successful social relationships. Good parenting teaches the child that give and take is the foundation of relationships and only then does the child have a chance at successful friendships throughout life.

This four part model does not require extensive training, it does not require the use of sophisticated technology, and it does not require taking a child to an expensive expert. What it does require is a smart, consistent and difficult (but doable) approach that in most cases will yield results.

There are times that either the child is too damaged or represents too great a risk to remain in the family. There are also times that parents have little or nothing left to give and are unable to apply steps like extending a genuine desire to connect with a child who has been consistently hurtful. At times like these it may be necessary to disrupt a negative pattern and remove the child from the home while professional attachment treatment is pursued.

It appears contradictory to some adults that attachment can be improved by removing a child from the home and placing him or her into a treatment program. After many years of treating young children with attachment issues in a residential setting, we have learned there are several logical reasons why the needed treatment outside the home can change a negative pattern between the child and parent.

- A consistent dynamic is that families give a great deal to the child and the child gives little or nothing in return. By removing the child from the home this pattern immediately stops--giving both the child and the parents a chance to develop interactions that can work.
- The child can now enter an entirely different environment that has high expectations of reciprocity, and the many tactics used by the child now do not work to get what they demand while giving little in return.
- Parents initially get a much needed rest and can heal the hurt that most have gone through with a child who has been so unresponsive in any positive respects.
- The child can begin to learn the give and take of relationships with hundreds of monitored social interactions throughout each day with a wide variety of peers and adults.
- A treatment setting can help to immerse the child in a setting where social skills must be learned before the child gets what is wanted, and children with attachment problems want many things.
- A residential setting allows the adults to work with the child in shifts and do not get worn down by the child's tactics to push others away.
- A residential setting also can facilitate the healing of complex trauma through intensive psychotherapy.

For these and other reasons, we have found that the treatment program at Jasper Mountain has been able to obtain consistently positive outcomes in the treatment of the most serious cases of attachment problems in young children.

Improvement in attachment is one of the most positive outcomes of the many areas we track in our treatment population.

Interventions to Repair Attachment

A number of years ago I put together what I called the building blocks of treating emotional disturbance, which generally involves attachment problems. The building blocks can be viewed as a therapeutic staircase that begins with the bottom step and progressively moves upward. The important aspect of the staircase analogy is that to be stable, stairs must be firmly established on the foundation of the step below. Thus, without *safety*, there is no attachment, no relationship, and no successful therapy that can occur. The stairs progress to *security* which is provided by consistent and predictable structure. This progression continues upward to *acceptance* on the part of the environment of who the child actually is, not just what their potential may be. The child must experience a *belonging* to the source of a potential attachment, although they will seldom acknowledge this feeling. *Trust* can only come after these preceding steps, and only then can a true *relationship* be available. It is in relation to another that we learn *self-awareness,* and only with self-awareness can *personal worth* blossom. Personal worth is definitely a higher order state, but it is important for attachment as an adult. For even when a person has learned to attach and to love, if they do not feel they are worthy of the love and attention of the beloved, they may eventually push the beloved away because they believe the other person deserves better.

Figure 1. Building Blocks of Treating Emotional Disturbance

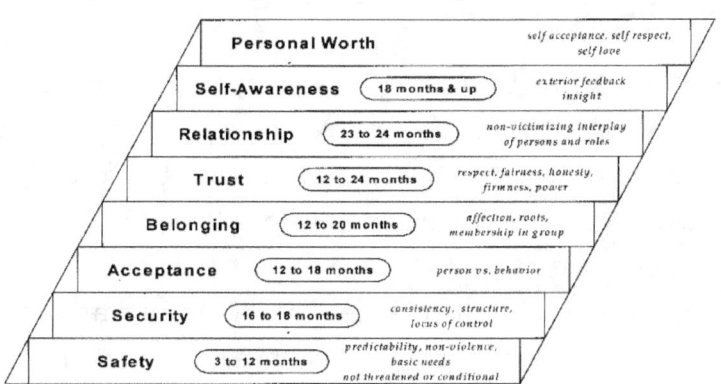

These building blocks have been found to be an invaluable framework in the clinical practice of the author's work for over two decades. It can be used to determine how far the treatment has progressed and what the next step should be. It can also be an important diagnostic tool to consider on what step a child enters treatment and how far up the stairs they have been able to go. A child is likely to be on a different step with each parent, teacher and therapist. She may be on the trust step with one parent and on the security step with the other parent. It is also important to point out the most common misconception of an inexperienced attachment therapist—believing they have a relationship with a child long before the essential steps have been reached.

▶ Use the "Building Blocks" to determine what step you are on with the child you are working with. Then ask yourself what actions you can take to improve the current step and move to the next step. A child will be on a different step with all the adults in his or her life. The goal is to move up the steps with as many adults as possible to improve relationship skills.

Attachment is Repaired not in a Professional Office but in the Entire Environment the Child Experiences

Attachment is repaired by a steady and consistent process of promoting, encouraging and even expecting positive connections with others. Attachment cannot be forced, but without positive encouragement it may not take root. A child who has been consistently hurt by an adult will not choose to be vulnerable again. Because safety is so important to the brain, it will choose safety over convenience, comfort, and even gratification. It is not unusual for children who have been traumatized to voluntarily undergo pain and humiliation if they believe the end result is safety. To a child who has been damaged by someone who they were instinctively drawn to connect with, the thought of being vulnerable to anyone else is a direct threat to safety. Only when the brain experiences the positive benefits of attachment without the threat of giving up safety and repeating this many, many times does the brain begin to first accept attachment and then pursue attachment with others.

Attachment is repaired by positive experiences of relationships, not by drugs, interventions or coercive treatments. The most effective attachment repair impacts all aspects of the child's life. It must be integrated, consistently positive, and include successful experiences to make the greatest difference. To further breakdown the process of repairing attachment there are a number of adjustments and goals to achieve in the child's environment that can be helpful.

- Consistent experience of safety – this is the foundation of any improvement. It is not enough that the environment is safe, the child must experience safety, and this involves adjusting the child's perceptions of the world he or she is living in.

- Predictable setting – most children love surprises, but not children who struggle with attachments because past surprises have largely been negative due to traumatic experiences. In every setting, the more predictable the surroundings the less stress for these children.

- Excitement and relaxation are present through the allostatic process – expression is a very important aspect of healing psychological scars. Allostasis can be best explained by comparing it to the more familiar homeostasis, meaning to stay within a narrow range of fluctuation. The temperature in a comfortable house stays within a desirable range often with the help of a thermostat. Allostasis broadens the range of familiarity and, when it describes emotional expression, it helps the child both increase and decrease emotional energy and become more able to experience and handle a broader range of emotions. Allostasis can help a child learn self-regulation as well as the ability to relax.

> ► Allostasis must be taught to the child. Each time a child becomes emotionally dysregulated, such as in a tantrum, this gives the adult an opportunity to teach the child to relax and calm down. Repeating this cycle teaches the child's brain that strong emotions can be handled and need not end in being hurt by the adult.

- Presence of support from multiple sources – early attachment begins with the physical and emotional caring and nurturance from one individual. The repair of attachment can be fostered with emotional support from a wide range of adults. Some people believe incorrectly that the goal in attachment work is to bond with only one primary care provider as a healthy infant first learns. However, when a child experiences many caring and nurturing adults, this can change the child's perceptions and speed up the process of experiencing the benefits of attachment without experiencing harm.

- Stimulating setting that promotes learning and accepts mistakes – the two main jobs of a child are to learn and to play. Children do both best when they experience an environment that is stimulating and fun. This is true both in the family and in their first step into the world away from home when they attend preschool or elementary school. Learning is not possible without making some mistakes. Children who avoid being vulnerable will often not attempt something new and risk failure. To help children learn the environment must accept and even celebrate mistakes because it means the child is trying and taking positive risks in order to learn.

- Childlike play is encouraged – once again play is one of the two primary jobs of a child. But childlike play is not what many adults consider it to be -- simply expending energy in childish activities so they can do better at meaningful work at home or in the classroom. Play is work for children. Play helps the body, mind and spirit. Children learn to express, they learn to forget their concerns and re-create themselves by lowering stress, improving their imagination, and learning social conventions and skills. Nearly everything a child must learn can be found in childlike play. The problem is that traumatized children lose the desire as well as the ability to play. It is therefore critically important to encourage childlike play.

> ► Play is not frivolous or a waste of time and energy, it provides many positive returns to the child. Play should therefore be encouraged, modeled and engaged in by adults with the child. Play should be a part of every treatment plan for a child with attachment problems.

- Expression is promoted in both genuine positive and negative forms – adults prefer the expression of positive emotions and try to reduce negative emotions. However, this is a mistake when repairing attachment. Emotions can be either positive or negative, but the most important indicator of attachment repair is that emotions be genuine. The first genuine emotions a child with attachment difficulties is likely to express are of the negative variety. If these negative emotions are discouraged by the adult, then expression, risk and connection are actually being discouraged. The key is to focus on how genuine the feelings are and promote honest expressions regardless of the content. For example, if a child is genuinely frustrated and in tears says, "I just want to die!" one response could be, "I appreciate you letting me know how you feel." After expression is encouraged, a gradual shift to more positive expression will be easier to achieve.
- Help the child experience the joy of life-long learning – the second job of a child is to learn. Since learning

involves risk and failure, the two most dreaded experiences for a child with attachment problems, then many kinds of learning are avoided by the child, particularly formal learning in school. Avoiding school is easier to identify than all the other ways these child avoid the risk of learning. They play by themselves in part because they do not want to risk social interaction. They do not try new things even when it is fun for other children such as swimming, riding a horse or trying a new activity. Broad exposure to learning opportunities should be encouraged to help the child experience the positive results such as the excitement and fun of life-long learning.

- Instruction of all desired skills with no assumption these skills will come naturally to the child – adults often believe that children naturally learn a wide range of skills such as empathy, remorse, and delaying gratification. The reason for this is they have the experience of children picking up ideas from their environment and learning skills they have not been taught. However, with traumatized children it is a different matter. These children are avoiding adults and suspicious of rules or trying something new and unfamiliar. These children must be specifically taught all skills they will need other than how to be self-protective and cautious, because these are the traits that come naturally on their own.

- Social skills are learned primarily through social inclusion – we learn best in interactions with others. Social inclusion is a potent force for learning. Traumatized children may avoid others and must be encouraged to be social and be a part of groups of people involved in an activity. If there is a choice between encouraging a child with attachment problems to do something solitary or something social, it will be the social experience that has the best chance of helping the child learn important skills.

> ▶ Some believe children struggling with attachment should only interact with an adult and should not interact with other children, particularly other children with similar problems. However, in the long run, preventing social contacts is shortsighted because of the learning that could take place. Encourage connection and social activities such as teams, clubs, and situations where there is ample social inclusion. Yes, the child will struggle, but all learning requires struggle.

- Allowing appropriate control through choices – traumatized children are often obsessed with control. Intense control issues come from early experiences of a serious lack of control combined with the experience of threat without being able to rely on adults for protection. Control can either become a power struggle with adults or alternatively the child can be given some choices through which she can experience appropriate control. Such choices may involve small matters, but they are often perceived as large to the child. She may be given a choice of three chores, or she may be allowed to pick a topic to study in school. The child could be given a choice of a bath before or after dinner or what color bed spread she would like to have. There are many ways a child can be given some level of control. Although it will likely never be enough control for the child, it is providing the child a sense of some appropriate control.

> ▶ Give the child appropriate control and choices over some aspects of his life, and ignore all the child's efforts to obtain control over everything else in the environment. You know why the child has this need, so simply understand it and do not react to it.

- The child has a chance to lead and teach and be the one who knows – being in the one down position, such as being the one who does not know as much as other people, is very difficult for traumatized children, even though this is the position all children are in. It will help if there are situations when the child can teach the adults or other children about something. It gives the experience of competence and self-respect. For example, look how much enjoyment children get from explaining to adults how their smart phones work.

- Modeling of empathy is provided – children with attachment problems are universally lacking in empathy. It is difficult to be considerate of the feelings and experiences of others if you have not been on the receiving end of empathy. Modeling is the most effective way to teach others, and the modeling of empathy must be consistent with an emphasis on empathy extended to the child.

- Vulnerability and interpersonal risk taking is modeled and encouraged – since children with attachment difficulties avoid vulnerability and risk at all costs, it will take specific attention to have the child experience these areas with a successful outcome. It is understandable why they do not want to be vulnerable, and yet no connection with others is possible without being exposed and vulnerable. Attachment will require risk, and risk is contrary to what the limbic region of the brain will want to do.

- Instilling moral reasoning and higher human aspirations through external executive functions – some of the last executive functions, or higher order processing in the brain, are moral and ethical reasoning. The average individual fully develops moral reasoning in the middle to late 20s. It could be even later in life, if ever, for individuals with attachment problems. Developing moral and ethical reasoning will require instruction and extra effort on the part of adults in the child's life. Adults must understand how illogical it is for a child with bonding problems to comprehend moral principles like being considerate of others, being of service to others, forgiveness, and allowing others to get something you want before you get yours. From a more primitive level of thinking, none of these actions make any sense, but from a higher level of reasoning they all promote connections with others. Many higher aspirational principles sound nonsensical to egocentric children and teens, so they must be encouraged to see the positive outcomes of thinking of others.

- Providing the experience of being connected to something greater than the self (relationship, family, team or Supreme Being) – this is at the core of many moral or aspirational organizations such as religions.

However, connection is pain to the child with attachment issues. Without connection the world is a lonely, frightening and hurtful place. This leads to the child's dilemma, choose the vulnerability of connection or the pain of isolation. To the child this is a losing proposition either way he or she chooses. However, with positive experiences of connection the brain can begin developing neuro-pathways of connection leading to pleasure, and over time this can make a major difference.

> ▶ The child's brain is an ally in the work to improve attachment--more specifically the brain's prefrontal cortex. It will first learn that connection offers many important advantages once it has consistent positive experiences. So think of all your efforts as directed to the part of the child's brain that will learn the quickest and do not get discouraged by the child's limbic reactive and resistant brain. The human brain is more like a committee than an individual, so focus on the member of the committee that has the best chance to understand that attachment is the answer to social success in life.

- Promoting direct experiences and discouraging vicarious experiences – an active fantasy life can be very healthy for a normal child. However, for children who have not had normal early development, fantasy can be a way to avoid social connections. Excessive reading, video games, TV watching and other pursuits that do not involve other people and take the child away from the world all around him or her may end up leading to avoiding connection with others. These pursuits can at times be more harmful than simply avoidance of others. Some books, music and video games can have themes of aggression, violence, revenge and other negative pursuits. The best plan is to encourage involvement with the real world and limit or restrict a passive spectator approach to life.

- An environment that is fun and filled with laughter – since the main job of a child is to learn and have fun, enjoyment is a major aspect of repairing attachment. When a child experiences fun there are many important processes taking place. Enjoyment helps to reduce stress and there are multiple physiological advantages to laughter and enjoyment, including dilation of arteries and improved circulation among many others. Fun with others begins to develop new mental maps connecting others with enjoyment. The child's prefrontal cortex will be attracted to fun. Social skills, pleasure, and learning are also enhanced by fun and laughter. If the home or the classroom are not places where there is frequent laughter, then an important element is missing in the world of the child with attachment issues and a helpful strategy is being overlooked.

- Modeling going beyond self to help others – children do not learn to think of others rather than themselves without witnessing this happening. Modeling has always been the most potent form of teaching. A child cannot bond with another person without experiencing someone caring enough to help the child. When the child experiences caring from others, it is easier to teach the child to help and care for others. The nature of attachment must include a give and take of going beyond the self and reaching out and caring for another.

- Recognizing small and large successes and accomplishments – it is the foundation of shaping behavior when approximations of desired behavior are recognized and reinforced. For a child who needs to learn to do well socially, it is important to let the child know when he or she is accomplishing the task at some level. It is a part of human nature that we tend to repeat what we are successful in doing, so reinforcing small and large successes are another form of teaching and shaping desired behavior.

All of the above promote the positive stimulation, development of the orbitofrontal cortex, experiencing the advantages of connection with others, and therefore encourage attachment.

What Am I Doing Right and What Should I Do Differently?

If you are still reading this, then there is a very good chance you have not given up believing that your child can form better attachment with you and others. If this is true for you then you are doing the first thing right, you remain hopeful. Even if you have your doubts whether the attachment will ever be with you, it is critical to remember that you are planting seeds of attachment that may not mature for years, and it will likely be someone else who reaps the direct benefits. However, there are few things as fulfilling as opening the door to social success for someone, when this is unlikely without the ability to be vulnerable and close to other people. Since you are still reading, then you are also probably looking for ideas that can help the difficult task you have, and this is the second thing that you are doing right—seeking ideas to improve your situation.

> ▶ Most adults who work with challenging children would do well to take a longer view of the goals and objectives. What will this child need to learn to be successful as a young adult? What must happen for her to be a good mother ten years from now? We cannot be too focused on short-term gains because success may be defined far in the future and not in the next few months.

If you have made it this far with your child and have not lost your marriage or your physical or mental health, then you must be taking care of yourself and this is another critically important thing that you are doing right. If you are reaching out for others to help you with your challenge, this is the right thing to do as well. Children with disrupted attachment need the help of many adults, both on a practical energy level as well as sending a message to the child's brain that there are many adults in the world who are supportive and potentially helpful--unlike early experiences with neglectful or abusive adults. Up to now you may not have received the help you were asking for or needed, but enlisting the help of other adults is the right thing to do in the short and long run.

There are a number of other right things to do, and hopefully you can relate to several of the following:

Pacing yourself – if you believe that improving your child's ability to bond to you and others will take considerable time, you are correct. Repairing attachment requires endurance, and you must do this work at a pace you can maintain for days, months and years. Slow and steady will not win on the race track, but it will win in this competition when you are competing with the child's brain networks that must be changed through consistent experience. It may be helpful to take the long view where you are putting in effort that will have maximum advantages years in the future. It is a lot to ask, but consider that you are planting a pecan or walnut tree and it will take 15 to 20 years before the fruits of your labor are fully appreciated. You are not only helping your child, but also helping the friends, partner and children of your child when you plant the seeds of attachment. Such effort is yet another example of parenting as practice at unconditional love, or giving without demanding an immediate return on your investment. If you can pace yourself in this hard work, you will have a better chance of maintaining your stamina for the long haul.

Not taking yourself too seriously – if you can still laugh, particularly at yourself, then you are doing something right. There is little that is fun or funny about running into a demanding and unappreciative child regardless of all you do for him or her. But even in the most challenging of times in life, it is the wise person who can see the irony, absurdity and humor in some of what is going on. Your child does not take you very seriously, why should you? I hope that brought a smile to your face! Well-adjusted and happy individuals are able to laugh at their troubles, and this is excellent modeling to help your child see someone who is not controlled by external factors.

Recharging your batteries – you are not expected to skip through your daily battles with your child laughing all the while. Much of what these children demand and put adults through is not funny. So periodically you have to take a break, remove yourself from the role of parenting for a period of time and recharge your energy and your spirit. Everyone is different, and what drains some people gives energy to others. So what will recharge your energy and enthusiasm is highly personal. There are a few standard energy restoring activities for most people such as: a good night's sleep, a weekend away, a good book, a dinner and movie out, and a solitary walk on a sunny day or on a beach. There are a limited number of times parents can get the space they might prefer, so don't put off taking care of yourself until your next two week vacation at a resort. Look for opportunities in each day for a few minute vacation and the brief chances to recharge and get ready for the next round with your child.

Understanding that you did not cause these attachment problems – you are not your child, and your child's failures, foul language, misbehaviors, and unpleasantness are not you. Parents can be too quick to take responsibility for the behaviors of their child, and this is not a wise thing to do with a child with attachment problems. It is difficult for nearly everyone to encounter a negative or even hostile person. When your child acts in a negative way toward others, you must quickly check your internal responsibility meter. You are not the cause of your child's problems, and it is important to remind yourself of this frequently.

Understanding that it took time to develop attachment problems, and it will take time to repair the damage – by now it should be clear that quick changes are neither possible nor desirable. A miracle cure would be great, but short of that the goal is long-term positive change in the child's brain. Such change is something that a quick fix cannot provide, because it takes time for the brain to form new pathways for all the positive changes we want the child to make. If we want the child to stop perceiving adults as threats, then it will take new neuro-networks to help the child create different perceptions. If we want prosocial behavior, positive emotions, willingness and even interest in being close to others, initiating making genuine contact with a parent and many other items on your wish list, then it will take time for the brain to respond differently. In the meantime you will just have to take care of yourself, invest more in your own mental health, and make sure you are enjoying as many aspects of your life as you can. So take a moment to thank your difficult child for teaching you the lesson of living as full a life as you can regardless of your challenges, it is an important lesson.

Seeing the frightened young child behind all the hostile or distant presentation – it is very easy to take the child with disrupted attachment at face value, but it is neither correct nor is it helpful. The external presentation of children with attachment problems is for show. Clearly it is not an enjoyable game of pretend for the child, and it would not have been the child's choice, but the child's brain is simply doing what it can for protection. Essentially all of the unpleasant symptoms of disrupted attachment are designed with one theme in mind — avoid the vulnerability of physical and emotional closeness by keeping others at a distance. I stumbled upon a cable TV episode of "The Dog Whisperer." In this show there was a tiny Chihuahua that had a difficult life in part because it was the most helpless creature everywhere it went. The way this vulnerable animal adapted to the life it found itself in was to become the 'demon dog.' It would rival a timber wolf in how ferocious it pretended to be. The Dog Whisperer, Cesar Millan, ignored the bluster, the snarling threats, and the bared teeth and came up close and held the animal as it attempted to fight back with all its strength. The dog did its best to first scare off the threat and then attempt to fight for its life. But Cesar held firm, and within a matter of a few minutes the primal struggle was over and both sides won. The Chihuahua calmed down and was not hurt; it quickly accepted the dominance order of being under the benevolent leader of the pack that happened to be a human. The remarkable side effect was the dog began to calm down with other adults as well once its brain had a new perception of being vulnerable but not hurt. As I watched this play out I realized he was facing the same thing parents face with children who are afraid of vulnerability. From this point on I was unable to see the dog as any type of demon or threat; it was simply a tiny creature just trying to get by. I tell this story because the next time you are snarled at by your child with bared teeth, I want you to see the tiny creature behind the bravado, because here too is someone just trying to get by and stay safe in a world full of the threat of vulnerability and helplessness.

> ▶ It is not just the child that needs some new perceptions. The adults need to look beyond the rough and unpleasant exterior of the child and see the scared and hurt child who is hiding behind all the bluster or indifference. If you can manage to do this it can be a game changer, because it is the frightened child with whom you want to connect.

If you are doing one or more of the above, then you are doing something right. Now take a look at a couple other things you have the power to change and add to what you are doing right. For each item that you struggle with there is an opportunity to make a change. Start small and give yourself credit when you have minor successes. This is a good place to enlist the help of a friend or coach. You can tell another person what your goal is, and then check in with them occasionally to give a progress report or ask for an idea. At the minimum, when we share our challenges with someone who is interested this makes our project more manageable, and we feel less stress due to the support we receive.

So what should you do differently? Any of the above that you are not doing now; do your best to make at least a small change in each of the areas.

Parenting 24 hours a day – if you are burned out then it is possible you have become stuck in the role of parent, and that will take all your energy away quickly. True, you can't just walk away from being a parent, but you are more than just a parent, and you need to put some attention into the other parts of your life and your interests: some alone time, exercise, taking a class, being a partner, investing in a hobby, or being a best friend to someone. Being more than a parent is one of the reasons that I discourage home schooling for children with disrupted attachments; you need a break, and frankly the child can use a break from you as well.

Giving until you have nothing left – you have to be aware enough to know when you have little left to give. No one comes out ahead when parents allow themselves to become totally depleted. The child will still be demanding, and you will need the energy to be patient. But if the energy is just not there anymore, bad things can happen. It is a good idea to check your reserves multiple times each day to catch an internal crisis before it becomes a serious problem. Consider a power nap, some of the best ways to recharge yourself are quick steps you can take at any time and any place. It may make it worse if you tell yourself you need a week or two on a beach somewhere to get your energy and endurance. Just like eating multiple times a day to feed our body, we must get some psychological and personal fuel several times a day as well.

Believing what the child says – so what do you hear frequently from your child? Do you hear some of these classics: "Whatever...I don't care... I hate this family...You don't care about me...I can't wait to get out of here...You are a terrible parent...You like to be mean...Why don't I ever get what I want," and more. The biggest mistake a parent can make is to take these statements at face value. It is a mistake because much of what they say is both untrue and the words do not convey the child's real message. Children with emotional disturbances use words for many reasons, but to convey an accurate message when under stress is usually not one of them. These children use words to get attention, get a reaction, to alleviate boredom, to confuse and perplex the adult, as magical thinking, and as self-protection, among others. A long time ago I noticed that teenagers and children with emotional disturbances often said the opposite of what their real message was, "I don't need your help," "I can live on my own at 13, just let me do it," "I don't need anything from you because I can take care of myself." I began saying the opposite to myself to see if that was closer to the real message, and then I responded to the accurate message while ignoring the words. I find children will be much more truthful with their non-verbal messages and the look in their eyes than any statement coming out of their mouths.

Sacrificing your marriage, or your physical or mental health – significant stress can produce many unfortunate internal and external impacts on parents who labor in vain to get closer to their child. It is important to monitor the impacts of the struggles you face. Be watchful of unresolved conflicts developing with your partner because many marriages have ended, in part, due to different opinions on raising a difficult child. There can also be other external stresses related to other children in the family, relatives who believe they know better ways to raise your child, and the judgments of friends and neighbors. So what do you tell your parents or your sister who give you unsolicited and unhelpful advice for your difficult child? My suggestion is that you tell them their support is very important, but your child is unique and you are following the parenting plan developed by the expert you are going to (you do have a professional coach to help you, right?). The internal stresses can impact your physical, mental and even spiritual health. Make sure you do your best to handle the stress. Remember that stress need not be the cause of overwhelming emotions and distress. It can be energizing and a sign that you need some extra support and help that you will listen to and follow up on.

Trying to go it alone – I have always considered parenting to be a team sport, and for children with attachment disturbances this is even truer. Even if you do not have a partner in parenting your child, you still could use a team to work with you such as a friend, a professional coach, the child's teacher, a pastor and perhaps a therapist for yourself who can help you monitor how positively you are handling your stress. If you do have a partner, then make sure you work together and avoid any possibility of the child driving a wedge between you. These children feel powerful if they can impact your relationship, don't let them.

Believing the doom and gloom predictions – there is actually a wealth of information you can find to work with children with disturbances of attachment. Not all of it is helpful or accurate. I have tried to point out approaches to avoid, and I will say more about this in the pages ahead. Some of the information on children with attachment problems is written to sell you something; other information is either overly optimistic or pessimistic. Ordering the internet special kit will not reverse attachment problems because only consistent brain changes can do this. On the other end of the continuum, it is not clear to me how it helps a parent to be told that their child with a disrupted attachment has a good chance of winding up a career criminal. But such statements are not hard to find, and they have little support in research.

Trusting in quick and easy cures – most parents of challenging children know better than to buy into a "new innovation" that is a quick and easy way to turn your child around. However, we all need hope and when parents are running out of ideas and energy, they are vulnerable to taking a risk, spending money, or signing up for something their common sense tells them is unlikely to make good on attractive promises. Parents cannot be blamed for getting to the point of desperation at times, but the quick cure may make things worse, at least in your bank account. Just remember the only repair for disrupted attachment is consistent efforts to promote positive brain change, and this is never quick or easy.

Believing the more expensive the treatment and the more technology involved the better – don't buy into the premise that the more expensive therapies are the most effective. We live in a society that holds technology in high regard. The medical care in the United States has the greatest use of advanced technology in the world and comes in as the most expensive — there is a direct connection. However, the overall health outcomes are worse than many nations that have a fraction of the cost. Technology and expense are not good predictors of healthy outcomes. Enterprising practitioners have developed ever increasing uses of technology to treat conditions like repairing attachment. But once again the cost and the use of advanced technology does not equate with positive outcomes. Two examples of the use of technology are neuro-feedback and brain scans. There is good science to support the use of neuro or bio-feedback. But this can be utilized at high or low cost and outcomes do not depend on the cost. Brain scans are becoming more popular and can be compelling to a parent. However, it is the resultant behaviors that tell us the most about brain deficiencies that need changing, and scans do not analyze behavior. Brain scan technology in its current form is best used for research and has very limited value in the treatment of a specific case.

The consumer must beware of the use of sophisticated technologies and references to research studies. The first question to ask is whether expensive technology can provide us with information not obtainable by observing the child. Another issue is whether the research findings done on a large number of individuals can have application to a particular child in a particular situation. An example of questioning the research can be seen in a surprising new study that was announced by the media on the day I was writing this section. The surprise to me was why they took the time and expense to do the research at all. The research question was whether brain scans could show deficiencies in the prefrontal cortex of convicted murderers. Since we know that the prefrontal cortex is involved in making good decisions, including moderation of aggressive and violent tendencies, I and many other psychologists could have saved the researcher time and said yes they would find prefrontal deficiencies in violent criminals, which was what they found. However, while the overall finding made logical sense (the part of the brain that assists in self-regulation was deficient in people with serious regulation problems), the researcher was quick to say the findings would be unhelpful in specific cases such as predicting if one individual would become a criminal. The reason for this was that while on brain scans most of the criminals had prefrontal deficiencies, the opposite was true for some criminals. For example the brains of sophisticated sociopaths reflected excellent prefrontal cortex functioning. So scans were helpful in answering a research question, but were not useful in predicting or treating murderers. In the same way brain scans of a large group of children may tell us some useful research information about the brains of large groups of individuals, but they would be of little use to understand and treat an individual child, despite claims that are made to the contrary.

So whether you are desperate or just making sure you leave no stone unturned to help your child, make sure you ask the right question when you hear advertisements designed to sound convincing such as:

➢ This new medication will make the difference for your child.
➢ The series of brain scans we offer will unlock the secrets of your child.
➢ Our two week intensive therapy will turn around your child.
➢ Our research has shown that following our regimen, now available at half price for a limited time only, will produce quick change in your child.
➢ We guarantee you will see a difference in your child after the first day.

To these and other similar tempting promises of the 'silver bullet' fix, you must ask one important question – will this provide reasons for the brain to make positive adjustments to making connections with others over an extended period of time? This question must be asked because it is the only route to repairing attachment. As you well know, what sounds too good to be true, probably is.

What to Do When Nothing Seems to Work

The starting place to discuss what to do when you are discouraged is to recognize that it is difficult to know when efforts to improve attachment are not working. It may not be difficult to see that a child is showing little or no interest in connecting with a parent, but even then improvement may need to be measured in small steps. At times a child may begin to show improvement in attachment not by how many times he or she initiates connections, but how many times the child may not object to the initiation of the parent. Physical touch can be one example of this where a child does not initiate physical touch but begins to reduce their objections to being touched by others. This is a small but important sign of improvement.

> ▶ Measuring the improvement in attachment involves the brain, so it is similar to other types of brain development such as learning to walk. There is no pill, technology or intervention that will cause a child to skip the required process of building up neuro- networks for balance and coordination. Walking takes time, considerable practice, and mastery. Just ask any stroke victim who has had to learn to walk all over again.

There is another complex factor that must be considered before determining that efforts to improve attachment are not working. In Part II the case was made that attachment at its most fundamental level is a neurological process. What we cannot see is how many internal brain changes are going on that may not immediately result in observable behavior. It is frequently the case that adaptations are taking place in the brain that will form the foundation of bonds and attachments at a later point. For example, when a child who has paid a price for getting close to an adult in the past has the experience that she is not hurt, and in fact there are some positive aspects to the connection with another person, the observable behavior may continue to reflect caution and rejecting connection, but the brain notes the positive rather than negative outcomes of the contact. Slowly, the neuro-mapping of networks in the brain grow stronger that connection does not equal pain and harm. As the ongoing process of adaptation takes place the child becomes gradually, and sometimes imperceptibly, more open to being close to others.

Children with attachment difficulties can be very good teachers to help adults learn about their own needs. We often must commit to a long-term process of helping a child with attachment difficulties for the sake of the child and not for ourselves. When we become frustrated, upset, and exhausted with the continual lack of consideration or appreciation from the child, it may not be about the child but about our own needs that we look to the child to meet--often unaware that we are doing so. These children are some of life's best teachers of unconditional love.

If adults are following the recommended model that has been outlined in this book (1. the child experiences a safe and secure environment, 2. insuring basic needs are unconditionally met, 3. invitations to connections repeatedly come from the adults and 4. reciprocity is taught by requiring an investment from the child if the child's many desires are to be met), there is a good possibility that important adaptations are happening in the child's brain. At times it helps to have an outside perspective to notice initial changes taking place, and this is the role of a coach.

A coach is someone who is external to the activity and because of experience and objectivity is able to see what may be hidden to the person being coached. A coach is not someone who is necessarily more skilled at the task. In the world of professional sports, seldom does the coach have more skill than the athlete being coached. The job of a coach is to observe the way that athletes are using their ability and to connect this to the outcome in order to suggest adjustments for improved performance. No one believes the batting coach could get more hits in the game than the professional players, but the role of the coach is to observe and make recommendations designed to maximize successful results. In the same way, a relationship coach is someone with the experience and objectivity to offer insights that would not necessarily be clear to the parent.

The coach need not be a paid professional. Friends, partners, a grandparent, or minister may be able to fulfill the role of a coach. The important requirement is objectivity, which at times is difficult for someone to have if there is a personal investment in the outcome. While the coach need not be a professional counselor, an experienced therapist is often a very good choice. Don't look for a professional who could do a better job with your child, but instead someone who can help you do a better job with your child.

One of the first steps of a good coach is to consider the health and resiliency of the parent. Children with attachment problems drain adults and can leave them worn out and burned out. No amount of insightful suggestions will help if the parent has no energy reserve. Even with children who can bond and attach, the job of a parent is to give and not always expect to receive in return. For a successful parent the return on the investment is precisely the reward of giving, supporting and loving the child. The successful parent does not always receive love back from the child, particularly when the parent's love requires that the child hear a "No" in response to a request. The highest reward for the good parent is doing the best job of parenting possible, regardless of the response from the child. There is a reason children cannot make all their own decisions and need parents to act in the child's best interests. Children want the immediate and short-term goal but parents must consider consequences and the long-term. Guiding the child with a long-term perspective is an important measure for parents of children with attachment problems. You must give yourself an accurate report card of your parenting, because the child and perhaps members of your extended family may well give you poor grades when, in fact, you are doing everything right.

It is a lot to ask of a parent to give unceasingly but not to expect much in return. This is one reason that parenting is considered the most difficult job in the world. There are very few other tasks that any of us perform continually when we get little or nothing back. So how can parents possibly be successful at unconditional love and investing in parenting when it seems only anger and a lack of appreciation are what comes back? There is only one sure method to avoid running out of the energy it takes to be a good parent and that is to insure you find ways to recharge your battery. Parents who cannot take a break will likely not maintain the pace very long. I mentioned earlier I recommend against home schooling for children with attachment problems, since the parent needs time away from a demanding child. It is not only a physical break that is necessary, but a mental break as well. An afternoon off, a day at the beach or a few hours with a good friend may not help if the parent is worrying what is going on with the child the whole time. To be a good parent we cannot be a parent every minute of the day. There are as many ways to recharge one's battery as there are parents who need to keep doing so. Exercise, painting, reading, meditation, volunteering, biking, gardening and any number of activities have been shown by research that they give back much more than we invest in these activities. Find what works best for you. One principle that must be mentioned is that it is not the child's job to give you energy, it is your responsibility. No car will run long without refueling, and parents will not succeed without refueling in a way that works for them.

Even if it feels like all your efforts have produced few positive results, it is critical to remember that the brain is always capable of making positive change that adapts to the environment. There is no question that early dispositions of avoiding attachment can become strongly habitual, but there is also no question positive adaptation is invited by showing a young person the advantages of support and reciprocal relationships, such as friendships, and how fun is increased by doing something enjoyable with a friend.

Another important point to consider is that even if a child does not show improved attachment at the time, there will be many times in life when he or she will have another opportunity. Nearly every developmental period of life can create conditions for a child's brain to reconsider the fundamental disposition allowing others to get close or pushing others away. This is because every developmental period of life requires social connections. One of the important times this can take place is in early adulthood. It is then that developmentally most people look for partners to share life's joys and trials. It can be at this time that the individual's brain questions the usefulness of separation. Even if the individual has arrived at this period in life without the social skills to take full advantage of a change in this fundamental disposition of getting close to others, the mental tension can produce important perceptual changes related to bonding with others.

The answer I offer to the question 'what to do when nothing seems to be working' is to take a step back and get some perspective, consider if there are changes you can make to promote better success, realize that you are planting seeds of attachment that may sprout and develop in the future, and make sure you take care of yourself and not allow parenting a child with serious attachment issues to deplete your reserves. If you have done your best in each of these areas and you find yourself depleted and not sure what to do, then get professional help or what I call professional coaching.

All Professionals Are Not the Same; Elements of the Help You Need

Professionally it gets a bit tricky to recommend seeking out certain therapists and avoiding others, but should it be a sensitive issue? If someone needs back surgery a doctor of chiropractic is not what someone needs. Likewise, if someone needs a spinal adjustment, a back surgeon is not the best answer. So it is not that one professional is better in all circumstances, it just depends on the situation. In the area of professional help, it may seem ironic but a professional who specializes in attachment may not be the best answer. The reason for this has to do with the complexity of the problem. The best treatment of attachment difficulties is an integrated, holistic approach, and not a packaged 'one size fits all' approach for just bonding issues. Specialists may be very versed in bonding problems, but at times this can get in the way when other issues are seen through the lens of the specialization. A professional or an organization that says they only do attachment work is probably not the best choice.

There are other specialists who may not be the right choice as well. Non-directive play therapy has a time and a place, but not to improve attachment. Non-directive work can be effective, particularly in understanding the client's internal perceptions. Play therapy can be a very impactful approach in many situations. However, what is needed to improve attachment is a very directive approach by having the child reach out and become vulnerable; exactly what he or she does not want to do. In this situation only a directive approach will move the child to where he or she needs to go.

Individual therapy has shown itself to be an effective intervention since the time of Freud's "talking cure." There is definitely a place for individual work in the area of attachment. But there is an exception. The role of the therapist includes deeply understanding the child and communicating ideas and information to the family. The type of individual therapy to avoid is when it is separated from the integration approach overall. Individual therapy to help with the overall treatment cannot shut out the parents by being "confidential" between therapist and child. In this case the word 'confidential' could be exchanged with 'secretive.' If an individual therapist insists upon not sharing with the parents what is going on in sessions with the child struggling with attachment, then another therapist is recommended.

One reason mental health professionals specialize in one area is that physical health doctors have done this for years, and it can be very lucrative. It is specialists and not generalists that make the most money in medicine and some therapists have noticed this trend. There are professionals and organizations that have found specializations in mental health work to be lucrative as well. Attachment centers around the United States have been started over the last three decades, and some have been very financially successful. While some are better than others, one theme to avoid with such services is the promise of quick results for a steep price. Every parent wants quick results, and most would pay extra to achieve this elusive promise. The problem is that it has taken time for the attachment difficulties to develop and it takes time for improvement. "Intensive" weekends or even weeks of focused therapeutic work mainly have an intensive impact on your bank account and cannot produce long-term progress. The brain can change but it does so incrementally and one situation at a time, there are no silver bullets that make this process quick, regardless of the cost.

Some organizations promise sophisticated technology such as brain scans. While brain scans have been found to be helpful in research on the brain, their use with directing treatment for individual clients may still be years in the future. The question to ask about sophisticated and expensive brain scans is what will a scan tell us that is not obvious to the trained eye in assessing and observing the child without such technology. In an era of advanced technology, it is tempting to want to have a picture of the brain. For the right price such a picture is available, but will it make a difference in what needs to happen to improve attachment remains a question.

There are some treatments that have been common and even popular in the past to treat attachment difficulties, but they should always be avoided. These approaches have been given a number of names such as "holding therapy" or any type of physically intrusive interventions. This caution does not include physical steps to prevent the child from harming self or others. There is a fundamental difference between the use of physical interventions when a child is violent and aggressive to self or others, and intentionally placing a child in a situation designed to cause pain, anger or physical coercion to facilitate attachment. Such an approach may, in fact, produce a bond, but it is much more likely to produce a harmful or trauma bond than a healthy bond. The brain of a child will sense threat and, at times, will go along to promote survival, but this is not a loving, comforting bond; it is a destructive, stressful connection with the source of threat. You cannot use pain as a means to promote vulnerability and stress reducing connection between people. To attempt to do so is working against the child's brain rather than offering the child's brain a better means of being successful.

Good treatment takes time, but more time is not always better. Pulling the plug on treatment after a few weeks is much too quick, but waiting years is much too long. A common question is how long should a treatment approach be given to show progress? One general guideline is if an integrated plan is not achieving a level of anticipated progress after six months, then it may be time to reassess the approach.

One last comment on treatments to avoid takes a page from financial scams. If the approach defies logic and does not seem to make good common sense, be sure to proceed cautiously because it may be exactly as it seems, too good to be true. When all is said and done, there is only one formula for improving attachment and that is to offer safety and ways for the child to experience positive connection in order for the child's brain to feel the value and to do this over an extended period of time. In this way the brain's neuro-pathways are developed and strengthened and gradually grow more dominant, while the prefrontal cortex experiences the positive benefits of attachment leading it to want more of what attachment brings. Only these important factors will produce positive brain change and genuine attachment.

How to Get the Most Value Out of This Book

You have now reached the end of this concise treatment of repairing attachment. But don't be done just yet with the ideas covered in all three parts. This was not meant to be a page-turner where you can't wait to find out 'who done it.' We all know who done it, it was the people who did not meet the early needs of the child you are working with, and now you have the challenge to do something about it. I certainly hope you found some suggestions that you want to implement. The second time you read the book (yes, it will take more than one reading, which is why I made it short and practical) I suggest you read 3-5 pages at a time. This will give you a chance to think over the concepts and put some to the test. Whatever you try that does not work, stop and move on to try another idea, since not everything will work with every child. After completing the second reading, you need to decide if taking any further steps will help you. If so, make a copy of the suggestions and put them prominently where you will see them, but not where the child sees them. Remember that it is not just the child's brain that must gradually change, so does yours. We all get into habits, and if any of these habits involve ineffective interactions with your child, then new neuro-pathways must develop within your brain to impact the child's brain.

I want to conclude the book by increasing the pressure you already feel--that if you don't help this child, then who will? I wish I did not need to emphasize this point, but I must. You know how hard it is for you to be around your child, now consider how hard it is to be the child and have to live in that world full time. Do you know what the odds are that your child will have a full and rewarding social life if nothing improves? About the same as becoming the dictator of a Central American country, after all they have many of the attributes and necessary skills! But seriously, without a social network and social support there is only a very slim chance of the child being happy and satisfied with the life ahead. You know how important it is that you do all you can at the child's present age to make a difference many years from now. On the days you don't know if you can do all that is required, remember how important it is that you are successful, and how many people you may be helping a few years down the road.

I am not asking you to keep giving for no return. If you get something back directly from your child, then appreciate it and count your blessings because many parents do not. However, the major return on your investment of so much effort to help your child is the internal satisfaction that you have done your part, and you have given so much and received so little in return. This is unconditional love and the highest level of living a life of service. Every major religion holds such a life up as a model to emulate and your child is making this possible.

If you never get an expression of thanks and appreciation from your child, then please accept it from me. I know what it takes from you and the difficulty of your challenge. Please also accept my support as you attempt to do the most difficult job on the planet—raising a child who has never learned to accept love from someone and give love back in return. There are heroes around us, and they are not athletes and celebrities, they are people just like you who work hard to help another person have a better life. Thank you for all you do for others.

References

Ainsworth, M.D.S., Blehar, M.C., Waters, E., & Wall, S. (1978). Patterns of Attachment: <u>A Psychological Study of the Strange Situation</u>. New Jersey: Lawrence Erlbaum Associates.

Ainsworth, M.D.S. (1979). Infant-Mother Attachment. <u>American Psychologist, 34</u>, 932-937.

American Psychiatric Association (2013). <u>Diagnostic and Statistical Manual of Mental Disorders, Fifth Edition</u>. Washington, DC: American Psychiatric Association.

Bates, J.E., & Bayles, K. (1988). Attachment and the Development of Behavior Problems. In Belsky & Nezworski (Eds.) <u>Clinical Implications of Attachment</u>. New Jersey: Lawrence Erlbaum Associates.

Belsky, J. & Cassidy, J. (1995). Attachment Theory and Evidence. In M. Rutter & D. Hay (Eds.), <u>Development Through Life</u>. London: Blackwell, 373-402.

Belsky, J. & Nezworski, T. (1988). <u>Clinical Implications of Attachment</u>. New Jersey: Lawrence Erlbaum Associates.

Bigler, E.D. (2001). Frontal Lobe Pathology and Antisocial Personality Disorder. <u>Archives of General Psychiatry, 58</u>, 609-611.

Bohlin, G., Hagekull, B. & Rydell, A.M. (2000). Attachment and Social Functioning: a Longitudinal Study from Infancy to Middle Childhood, <u>Social Development, 9(1)</u>, 24–39, 2000.

Bowlby, J. (1982). Attachment. New York: Basic Books Inc.

Caspi, A., Elder, G.H. & Bem, D.J. (1987). Moving Against the World: Life Course Patterns of Explosive Children. Developmental Psychology, 23, 308-313.

Cavada, C. & Schultz, M. (2000). The Mysterious Orbitofrontal Cortex. Cerebral Cortex, 10(3), 205.

Crittenden, P.M. (1981). Abusing, Neglecting, Problematic, and Adequate Dyads: Differentiating by Patterns of Interaction. Merrill-Palmer Quarterly, 27, 1-18.

Dallaire, D.H. & Weinraub, M. (2007). Infant-Mother Attachment Security and Children's Anxiety and Aggression at First Grade, Journal of Applied Developmental Psychology, 28(5-6), 477–492.

Erickson, M., Sroufe, A. & Egeland, B. (1985). The Relationship Between Quality of Attachment and Behavior Problems in Preschool in a High-Risk Sample. Monograph for the Society for Research in Child Development, 50, 147-166.

Felitti, V.J., Anda, R.F., Nordenberg, D., Williamson, D.F., Spitz, A.M., Edwards, V. & Koss, M.P. (1998). The Relationship of Adult Health Status to Childhood Abuse and Household Dysfunction. American Journal of Preventive Medicine, 14, 245-258.

Fonagy, P. (2000). Attachment and Borderline Personality Disorder. Journal of the American Psychoanalytic Association, 48(4), 1129-1146.

Gaensbauer, T.J. & Hiatt, S. (1983). Facial Communication of Emotion in Early Infancy. In N. Fox & R. Davidson (Eds.) <u>Affective Development: A Psychobiological Perspective.</u> New York: Erlbaum.

George, C. & Main, M. (1979). Social Interactions of Young Abused Children: Approach, Avoidance and Aggression. <u>Child Development, 50</u>, 306-318.

Granot, D. & Mayseless, O. (2001). Attachment Security and Adjustment to School in Middle Childhood, <u>International Journal of Behavioral Development, 25(6)</u>, 530–541.

Greenspan, S.I. & Lieberman, A.F. (1988). A Clinical Approach to Attachment. In J. Belsky & T. Nezworski (Eds.) <u>Clinical Implications of Attachment</u>. New Jersey: Lawrence Erlbaum Associates.

Herman, J.L. (1992). <u>Trauma and Recovery</u>. New York: Basic Books Inc.

Hershberg, L.M. & Svejda, M. (1990). When Infants Look to their Parents: Infants' Social Referencing of Mothers Compared to Fathers. <u>Child Development, 61</u>, 1175-1186.

Jablonka, E. & Raz, G. (2009). Transgenerational Epigenetic Inheritance: Prevalence, Mechanisms, and Implications for the Study of Heredity and Evolution. <u>Quarterly Review of Biology, 84(2)</u>: 131-76.

James, B. (1994). <u>Handbook for Treatment of Attachment-Trauma Problems in Children</u>. New York: Lexington Books, Macmillan Inc.

Kochanska, G. (1991). Socialization and Temperament in the Development of Guilt and Conscience. Society for Research in Child Development, 62, 1379-1392.

Kochanska, G. (1993). Toward a Synthesis of Parental Socialization and Child Temperament in Early Development of Conscience. Society for Research in Child Development, 64, 325-347.

Kohlberg, L., Levine, C. & Hewer, A. (1983). Moral Sages : A Current Formulation and a Response to Critics. Basel, New York: Karger.

Kubzansky, L.D., Sparrow, D., Vokonas, P. & Kawachi, I. (2001). Is the Glass Half Empty or Half Full? A Prospective Study of Optimism and Coronary Heart Disease in the Normative Aging Study. Psychosomatic Medicine 63, 910–916.

Laible, D. (2007). Attachment with Parents and Peers in Late Adolescence: Links with Emotional Competence and Social Behavior, Personality and Individual Differences, 43(5), 1185–1197.

Lewis, M., Feiring, C., McGuggog, C. & Jaskir, J. (1984). Predicting Psychopathology in Six-year-olds from Early Social Relations. Child Development, 55, 1123-1136.

Lieberman, A.F. & Pawl, J.H. (1988). Clinical Applications Of Attachment Theory. In J. Belsky & T. Nezworski (Eds.) Clinical Implications of Attachment. New Jersey: Lawrence Erlbaum Associates.

Liebeskind, J. (1991). Pain Can Kill. Pain, 44, 3-4.

Matos, L., Arend, R.A. & Sroufe, L.A. (1978). Continuity of Adaptation in the Second Year: The Relationship Between Quality of Attachment and Later Competence. Society for Research in Child Development, 49, 547-556.

Polansky, N.A., Gaudin Jr., J.M., Ammons, P.W. & Davis, K.B. (1985). The Psychological Ecology of the Neglectful Mother. Child Abuse and Neglect, 9, 265-275.

Raine, A., Melroy, J.R., Bihrle, S., Stoddard, J., LaCasse, L. & Buchsbaum, M.S. (1998). Reduced Prefrontal and Increased Subcortical Brain Functioning Assessed Using Positron Emission Tomography in Predatory and Affective Murderers. Behavior Science Law, 16(3), 319-32.

Rubin , K.H. & Lollis, S.P. (1988). Origins And Consequences Of Social Withdrawal. In J. Belsky & T. Nezworski (Eds.) Clinical Implications of Attachment. New Jersey: Lawrence Erlbaum Associates.

Schneider, B.H., Atkinson, L. & Tardif, C. (2001). Child-Parent Attachment and Children's Peer Relations: a Quantitative Review, Developmental Psychology, 37 (1), 86–100.

Schore, A.N. (1994). Affect Regulation and the Origin of the Self: The Neurobiology of Emotional Development. Mahweh, New Jersey: Erlbaum.

Schore, A.N. (2003). Affect Regulation and the Repair of the Self. New York: W.W. Norton.

Shaw, D.S. & Vondra, J.I. (1995). Infant Attachment Security and Maternal Predictors of Early Behavior Problems: A

Longitudinal Study of Low-Income Families, Journal of Abnormal Child Psychology, 23(3), 335–357.

Spangler, G., Schieche, M., Ilg, U., Maier, U., & Ackermann, C. (1994). Maternal sensitivity as an external organizer for biobehavioral regulation in infancy. Developmental Psychobiology, 27, 425-437.

Sroufe, L. A. (1986). The Role of Infant-Caregiver Attachment in Development. In Belsky & Nezworski (Eds.) Clinical Implications of Attachment. New Jersey: Lawrence Erlbaum Associates.

Steele, H. & Steele, M. (2008). Early attachment predicts emotion recognition at 6 and 11 years. Attachment and Human Development, 10, 379-393.

Trevarthen, C. (1998). Explaining Emotions in Attachment. Social Development, 7, 269-272.

Trickett, K. T. & Kuczynski, L. (1985). Children's Misbehaviors and Parental Discipline Strategies in Abusive and Nonabusive Families. Developmental Psychology, 22, 115-123.

Van Ijzendoorn, M.H. (1997). Attachment, emergent morality, and aggression: toward a developmental socioemotional model of antisocial behaviour, International Journal of Behavioral Development, 21(4), 703–727.

van der Kolk, B.A. (1989). The compulsion to repeat the trauma: Re-enactment re-victimization, and masochism. Psychiatric Clinics of North America, 12, 389-406.

Wittling, W. & Pluger, M. (1990). Neuroendocrine hemisphere asymmetries: salivary cortisol secretion during lateralized viewing of emotion-related and neutral films. <u>Brain and Cognition, 14</u>, 243-265.

Wittstein, I.S., Thiemann, D.R., Lima, J., Baughman, K.L., Schulman, S.P., Gerstenblith, G., Wu, K.C., Rade, J.J., Vivalacqua, R.J. & Champion, H.C. (2005). Neurohumoral Features of Myocardial Stunning Due to Sudden Emotional Stress. <u>New England Journal of Medicine, 252</u>, 539-548.

Zeanah, C.H., Smyke, A.T. & Dumitrescu, A. (2002). Attachment Distubances in Young Children II: Indiscriminate Behavior and Institutional Care. <u>Journal of the American Academy of Child and Adolescent Psychiatry, 41(8)</u>, 983-989.

Zeanah, C.H., Smyke, A.T., Koga, S. & Carlson, E. (2005). Building Attachment Relationships Following Maltreatment and Severe Deprivation. In Berlin, Ziv, Amaya-Jackson & Greenberg (Eds.) <u>Interventions to Enhance Attachment</u>. New York: The Guilford Press, 95-216.

Zeanah C.H. (2000). Disturbances and disorders of attachment in early childhood. In Zeanah (Ed.) <u>Handbook of infant mental health (2nd Ed.)</u> New York: Guilford Press, pp. 358-362.

Ziegler, D.L. (2004). Attachment Disorder Assessment Scale--Revised. Phoenix: Acacia Publishing.

www.ingramcontent.com/pod-product-compliance
Lightning Source LLC
Chambersburg PA
CBHW060148300526
45790CB00014B/370